Household EcoTeam Workbook

By David Gershon and Robert Gilman

Illustrated by Cynthia Fisher

Through this program you can do your part to achieve the global environmental goals in Earth Day's "Agenda for the Green Decade." These are the goals scientists have told us we each must achieve for the Earth to be on a sustainable path.

By achieving these goals, an average household of four will save *each year*:

- ◆ $1,200
- ◆ 3,120 lbs of garbage
- ◆ 104 cubic feet of landfill
- ◆ 10 trees
- ◆ 73,000 gallons of water
- ◆ 140 lbs of acid rain pollutants
- ◆ 10 tons of CO_2 emission
- ◆ 600 gallons of gasoline

all while improving their quality of life!

ISBN 0-9630327-0-4

Global Action Plan for the Earth
84 Yerry Hill Road
Woodstock, New York 12498 USA
Phone: 914/679-4830
FAX: 914/679-4834

Cover and interior pages printed on recycled paper with soy based inks.

Table of Contents

Acknowledgments

The creation of a work like this obviously draws upon many sources to come into form. First and foremost, we would like to acknowledge all those who have come before and dedicated their lives to saving our fragile and precious Earth from environmental destruction.

We offer heartfelt appreciation to the many who contributed to this creation:

- Cray Research for their financial support and pioneering development of GAP's Global Environmental Feedback System.
- Cynthia Fisher, Earth Day Publications, and *New Age Journal* for the use of Cynthia's illustrations.
- Jan Hanhart for the Ecofeedback and EcoTeam concepts.
- Kate Boyer, Marguerite Culp, Thomas Dooley, Duane Fickeisen, Doug Hines, Danny Mack, and Jay Nelson for assistance in the editing, design and production of this workbook.
- Lawrence Bloom, Fred Matser, and Virginia Fowler for their belief in GAP translated into practical support.
- Kathleen Gildred for her diligent research and collation of global environmental goals.
- Robert Carpenter, Daniel Chiras, Brando Crespi and George Kaufman for reading through this text and offering insightful feedback.
- All participants in the pilot program for their constructive feedback to help make this program as useful as possible.
- Denis Hayes and Teresa McGlashan of Earth Day for their inspiration and collaboration on the global environmental goals – "The Agenda for the Green Decade".
- Noel Brown, North American Director of UNEP, for his encouragement and support of GAP right from its infancy.
- Hazel Henderson for her insight into the environmental change process.
- The GAP Team for having the courage to both hold the vision and dedicate their lives to make it a reality.
- The *Fire In The Soul* training participants for their enthusiasm, spirit and encouragement.
- Finally, our wives, Gail Straub and Diane Gilman, for their continuous love, encouragement and help in grounding these ideas.

Getting Started

In this section:

About the Household EcoTeam Program

Where do I start?

The Household EcoTeam Program will help you translate your intention to do the right thing into a program of effective action.

If you're like many people, you have a vague sense of what you should be doing to restore the environment but you don't know where to begin. You probably feel overwhelmed. Or you may have gone as far as you know how and you need support to take the next step. You may be asking yourself questions like:

- Where do I start?
- Which actions are the important ones?
- Which of these should I take?
- How do I implement these actions?
- How does what I do actually make a difference?

The Household EcoTeam Program will assist you in translating your desire to do the right thing into a program of environmental action that will make a difference.

What it is – A six-month program to help bring your household into environmental balance. It simplifies the overload of environmental information into six sets of actions to be implemented, one set a month, with the support of a small group of friends, family members, or neighbors – your EcoTeam.

How it works – The primary components are:

- a small group of people supporting each other in making environmental changes within their household
- an easy-to-use workbook that walks you through a series of actions to move your household toward environmental balance.

Leverage – Your EcoTeam is one of many such groups operating all over the world as part of the Global Action Plan for the Earth (GAP). The results of actions by all the EcoTeams are collected at a central point and then communicated back to your EcoTeam. Each of your actions is keyed into Earth Day's "Agenda for the Green Decade" – the critical goals we need to achieve to restore our Earth's environment.

GAP is designed to empower us by showing how our individual actions are having a global impact, and how it is pre-

cisely through individual and local action taking place all over the world that we can achieve the global environmental goals necessary to sustain the quality of life on our planet. As the number of EcoTeams expands, the collective results will be significant positive environmental change.

Program components

Briefings

Many EcoTeams will be formed as a result of public presentations by members of GAP, called briefing sessions, which describe the EcoTeam and the Global Action Plan for the Earth. The *Household EcoTeam Workbook* is made available at the briefing, and individuals who want to form EcoTeams after hearing the briefing are encouraged to do so with the help of the workbook. It is also possible you will be made aware of the EcoTeam Program informally through contact with someone in the program, through an organization you belong to, through your workplace, or through the media.

Action Areas

Over a period of six months EcoTeam members help each other bring their lives into environmental balance and make an impact on global environmental goals (described in brief on page 5 and in detail starting on page 134) through working in six action areas:

- ◆ Reducing Your Garbage
- ◆ Improving Home Water Efficiency
- ◆ Improving Home Energy Efficiency
- ◆ Improving Transportation Efficiency
- ◆ Being an Eco-wise Consumer
- ◆ Empowering Others.

Process

Within each action area, the EcoTeam participants follow a similar process each month:

- ◆ Assessing your situation. What is your current environmental impact and how does it need to be changed?
- ◆ Performing the specific actions that will allow you to move toward environmental balance, whether it is a simple change in your house you can do right away or the first steps for a larger project that will take more than a month to complete.
- ◆ Reassessing your situation to find out how much your actions have moved your household toward environmental balance.

This is accomplished through a monthly meeting of the EcoTeam, designated weekly actions that support the goal you have set for yourself, and a weekly phone check-in with your EcoTeam coach to report results and learn how other members of your team are doing.

The monthly EcoTeam meeting begins with an acknowledgment of what took place the prior month and then introduces the action area for the coming month. This introduction includes a hands-on demonstration (such as a tour around the house where the meeting is being held) of the specific actions to be undertaken that month. During the whole process EcoTeam members are encouraged to be aware of and make inner changes in attitude as well as outer changes. For example considering how our thinking contributes to a "throw away" society as well as learning how to recycle.

In these six months EcoTeam members will have accomplished the essential initial steps required to bring their lives and homes into environmental balance.

During the whole process EcoTeam members are encouraged to be aware of and make inner changes in attitude as well as outer changes.

And they will have put in place for the long run the environmentally friendly lifestyle required of each of us to restore our larger home – the Earth – to balance.

How to Use this Workbook

Through this program you can accomplish the essential initial steps required to bring your household into environmental balance.

1) Use it as part of an EcoTeam. While the information in this workbook could be helpful to a single household or individual, you will have a better chance of success (and a lot more fun!) by using it as it was designed to be used: as one part of the full EcoTeam Program.

2) *Read the appropriate sections and chapters before each EcoTeam meeting.* We suggest that you read all of this "Getting Started" section before your EcoTeam meets for the first time. "Getting Started" and later chapters include notes for Eco-Team coaches. Wherever you find such material in the workbook, you are free to skim or skip it (if you aren't the coach), but reading it will deepen your understanding of the EcoTeam process.

Read over "Month 1: Reducing Your Garbage" in the "Household Environmental Action Areas" section before your first meeting. It is important to always read over the next action chapter before your monthly meeting.

3) *Take it month by month to avoid being overwhelmed.* Once you have begun the program, it is easiest to deal with only one month at a time. The program was designed specifically so that you could take it in bite-sized chunks.

4) *Use all the tools that each chapter provides to achieve full results.* The checklists, savings estimators, worksheets, and reporting forms are especially important. They are critical to both your success

and to GAP's ability to provide accurate feedback on the progress EcoTeams are making in this country and around the world. If you have any difficulty working with these, get help from your EcoTeam mates.

5) *Read "Our Big Picture" to understand the full impact of your actions.* The last major section of the workbook contains material on GAP's overall strategy, the basis for the global goals, other GAP programs, and related information.

6) *Recognize that the changes discussed in the EcoTeam Program will take time.* It's a human tendency to feel guilty if we don't do everything at once, yet it takes time to change a lifetime of habits. Some things you may want to do may not be presently available in your community and you'll have to compromise. Some choices will require a tradeoff. Be flexible and creative and, most of all, patient with yourself and others. How we walk the path of living in right relationship to the Earth is as important as being on the path. It's a lifelong journey, important to be taken seriously, but not so seriously that we can't laugh at ourselves regularly.

7) *Enjoy it.* This program provides an opportunity for you to develop rich friendships with your teammates as you work to support each other's efforts.

Global Environmental Action Goals
To be Achieved by the Year 2000

At the heart of the Global Action Plan is the following set of environmental action goals for the 1990s. The actions you will take as part of an Eco-Team will enable you to do your part toward the achievement of these goals.

The GAP team worked with the organizers of Earth Day 1990 to formulate this set of global goals, goals that need to be achieved in the next decade in order for the world to enter onto a path of environmental sustainability. What was created and launched by the organizers of Earth Day 1990 was the "Agenda for the Green Decade." These global action goals have the following purposes:

1) To enable us to know in quantifiable terms what we have to achieve over the next decade to protect the health of our environment.

2) To enable us to have reference points for developing and then measuring the progress of our actions.

The chapter, "Agenda for the Green Decade: Global Environmental Action Goals" starting on page 133 describes the background for these goals. Here we introduce these goals in summary form so that you can understand the larger basis for this program.

Preserve the Climate and Atmosphere

- Decrease carbon dioxide emissions by 20% through increased energy efficiency and increased use of renewable energy sources to slow global warming
- Eliminate emissions of and production of CFCs and other ozone depleting chemicals
- Decrease emissions of sulfur dioxide by 90% and nitrogen oxides by 75% to abate acid rain
- Improve urban air quality in the world's cities by reducing all automobile pollutants at least 50%.

Preserve Biological Diversity

- Triple the area of protected ecological preserves for species preservation
- Reduce deforestation by 50%
- Increase reforestation enough to offset deforestation by planting 100 billion trees
- Shift 50% of agricultural production to low-input sustainable agriculture. Reduce global pesticide use by 75%.

Reduce Waste

- Reduce solid waste by 75% through recycling, source reduction and composting
- Cut the production of hazardous waste by 80%
- Clean up all existing toxic, hazardous and nuclear waste sites to acceptable levels of safety.

Use Water Wisely

- Reduce water use by a third or more through more efficient use in agriculture, industry, and households
- Provide safe drinking water for all.

Stabilize Humanity

- Reduce the rate of world population growth by 50%
- Eliminate hunger.

Forming Your EcoTeam

Building The Team

By doing their part to achieve Earth Day's Agenda for the Green Decade, an average household of four will save *each year:* 3120 lbs of garbage, 104 cubic feet of landfill, 10 trees, 73,000 gallons of water, 140 lbs of acid rain pollutants, 10 tons of CO$_2$ emission, and 600 gallons of gasoline – all while improving their quality of life!

1) Your EcoTeam starts by you or someone else hearing about the program and taking the initiative to create an EcoTeam.

- The EcoTeam can be a combination of friends, family members, neighbors, colleagues or part of an already existing group or organization.

- The program is for everyone – homeowners and renters, adults and children – anyone who wants to take positive action for the environment.

- A good size is about eight to twelve members. This size range allows for both diversity and personal support for each member of the group.

- The EcoTeam can be composed of representatives of many households or all the members of just a few.

- If you live in a multi-household building, consider involving some of your neighbors in your EcoTeam so that you can work together on bringing your "larger household" into environmental balance.

2) Consider the following in forming your EcoTeam.

- Who in your life would you like to associate with regularly?

- Which of these people has a desire to be more environmentally sensitive? Many people today desire to be environmentally responsible and just need a little support to translate this into action.

- Appeal to each person based on their individual interests. Some possible reasons for participation might be:

  –to become environmentally responsible

  –to learn how to save money – our estimate is that by doing the actions in this workbook an average household could save a minimum of $300 per person per year

  –to make a positive difference by how you live your life

By doing the actions in this workbook, an average household could save more than *$300 per person per year.*

–to safeguard your health and that of your family

–to be part of a community

–to have fun

–to be part of a global, citizen-initiated movement that is substantially improving the environment

–to come into right relationship with the Earth.

3) Engage the support of the other members of your household so that you can all work together. This is *very* important because your whole household will be creating a new lifestyle. With everyone's cooperation throughout and after the program, the process will be more fun and less work. It makes sense to consider the *household* as the member of the EcoTeam and whoever attends the monthly meetings as the *representative* for the household (a role that could rotate).

4) Use this section of the workbook to explain the concept of the EcoTeam and how the program works.

5) Check schedules and arrange the time and place for the first meeting. To avoid future scheduling conflicts it would be wise to arrange the six monthly meeting times as you're arranging this initial meeting. You'll need approximately three hours for an EcoTeam meeting.

6) Before the first meeting each member should get a copy of the EcoTeam Workbook (directly or through you) and become familiar with its contents. Workbooks are available from your GAP Coordination Office, whose address can be obtained from the GAP National Coordination Office.

Initial Meeting

After you have formed your EcoTeam, the next step is to meet as a group to begin the program. The purposes of this initial meeting are to begin building relationships in the group, and to establish procedures for how the group will function. (You may also choose to begin work on the first environmental action area at this initial meeting, see sidebar). The following guidelines are intended to help you accomplish those goals:

1) Choose someone to facilitate (that is, chair or lead) the meeting. The person who initiated the group would be a good candidate for this first meeting. (In keeping with the EcoTeam idea we will call this person the "coach.") For facilitation guidelines, see following section: "Facilitating an EcoTeam Meeting."

2) Have each person share their reason for joining the EcoTeam and what they would like to gain as a result of their participation.

3) Based on what was communicated, clarify the purpose of the group. It may help to write this statement of purpose on a large sheet of paper so the whole group can see it clearly. Use this purpose statement to keep meetings on track.

4) Solicit commitment from team members to follow the program, attend the monthly meetings, provide weekly feedback punctually, and be on time for the meetings. To achieve practical results, it is essential for everyone to take their participation seriously. A clear and realistic commitment from each person garnered in this first meeting will assure everyone that the process will work.

5) Establish expectations for interpersonal communications that allows for

Some Eco-Teams begin work on the first environmental action area (garbage) at the initial meeting, while others prefer to wait until a subsequent meeting a week or two later. It all depends on how tight people's schedules are and how well they know each other. Do whichever works best for your team.

individuals to freely share both content and group process issues. To do this, solicit from the group what factors facilitate maximum participation. Create your guidelines based on this and also be open to experimenting once the process begins to unfold.

6) Determine how you want to make decisions as a group – consensus, majority rule, decision of the monthly coach, combination, etc.

Use page 11 to record team member's names and meeting dates.

7) Decide who will facilitate upcoming meetings. Many EcoTeams have found it helpful to divide up the facilitation (or coaching) for the five remaining monthly meetings among the different members of the EcoTeam. You might do this based on the interest of individuals in the action area. The responsibilities include facilitating the monthly meeting and weekly two-way communication of results achieved.

8) Set up logistics for your future meetings: location, day, length of meeting. Use page 11 to record this information as well as a list of team members' names, addresses, and phone numbers.

9) Either begin working on the first environmental action area, or meet again in a week or two to do so.

Facilitating an EcoTeam Meeting

The key to the EcoTeam Program is support. This section provides guidelines for facilitating monthly meetings in a way that supports motivation to take action through:

◆ an easy-to-use program

◆ encouragement from others.

If you had enough motivation on your own you would already have implemented the actions outlined in this workbook. The reason most of us have not done this isn't a lack of desire: it's that the required actions seem overwhelming and we don't know where to begin. In other words, we lack the needed support to take action.

The purpose of the coach in the monthly EcoTeam meeting is to provide his or her teammates with the necessary support to achieve the monthly actions. This is done in two ways:

◆ designing the monthly meeting to be inspiring and informative so your teammates are motivated to take action.

◆ maintaining inspiration throughout the month by serving as a weekly coach. Specifically this means obtaining weekly progress reports from each team member and then communicating back to each person the collective results.

Possible format for the meeting:

This section provides suggestions for the format of your monthly meeting. Additional information is provided in each monthly chapter (see "Notes for the Coach"). We suggest:

1) Starting with something inspirational and reflective that reinforces the purpose of the EcoTeam and provides

Since our beliefs determine our actions, it's essential to examine and reframe those beliefs that disable us.

motivation – poem, video, meditation, music or ceremony to connect with the Earth and each other.

2) Communicating the status of other EcoTeams to enhance motivation and build the sense of a larger community. (In the week prior to your EcoTeam meeting, contact your GAP Coordination Office to get an update on GAP.)

3) Having each person share their experience from the previous month. Consider dividing it into three parts:

- the practical results achieved
- personal insights, such as more awareness of impact of different actions on the environment
- the internal and external challenges that may have been experienced.

Include resistances to doing the action such as not managing time well or lack of motivation. Ask each person to communicate how, if at all, they might like support from the group in working with their challenges.

If a major resistance is identified, first ask the person to explain the belief underlying their action. An example might be: A team member didn't do any of the actions that month because work took up all his or her time. If this person's underlying belief were made conscious, it might sound something like –

"Work is more important to me than carrying out environmental actions around my house."

Then ask the person to find another way to view the situation that allows them to turn around or reframe the previous limiting belief. Ask them to phrase this as a belief. An example might be:

"Work is important to me and so is living in environmental balance. I repriori- *tize my time so that I live in harmony with the Earth."*

Another example of a limiting belief might be:

"I get overwhelmed when I have to do any calculations."

A turn around might be:

"I ask for help from my teammates when I need it."

The coach's responsibility is to help the person uncover the limiting belief and then reframe it. We often think in "either/or" terms. Reframing can help a person to think in "both/and" terms. Since our beliefs determine our actions, it's essential to examine and reframe those beliefs that disable us. If a team member is stuck, invite the rest of the EcoTeam to help uncover the belief and reframe it.

4) After each person has had a turn, which will take a while, particularly in the first few meetings, move on to the action item for the month.

- Educate your team members as to why this action is important. This creates the motivation to act. Use the first subsection in the action chapter, which provides background on the topic, to help you. If you need to, supplement this by referring to our Bibliography. Find a creative way to communicate this information. It will be more fun for you and your team.

- Review the sub-section in the action chapter entitled, "Action Opportunities" and choose several to demonstrate which you think will be most useful to your EcoTeam. You may also come up with other ideas. The purpose of this part of the meeting is to provide hands-on experience of some actions to be done that month. Practice in advance the actions you will be

Start with something inspirational and reflective that reinforces the purpose of the EcoTeam.

demonstrating so you understand them and are comfortable answering questions.

♦ Go over the monthly goal and ask each member of the team for a commitment to achieve this goal. If there are resistances, work them out so you can get agreement. If necessary modify the goal for those team members who have special needs that month. The key is to create wholehearted participation. Anything less is a drain on everyone's enthusiasm.

It is important for each household representative to fully explain each month's program to the rest of his or her household and gain their agreement for any actions undertaken.

♦ Then go over the section "This Month's Action Plan." Make sure everyone knows what weekly action is expected of them and what specifically to communicate to you. Get firm agreement with your teammates on the dates when they will phone you with their results. Select a day following this when you will provide feedback with the collective results achieved to your teammates. This ongoing communication is a very important part of the feedback process that has proven essential for sustaining the motivation of your EcoTeam.

At the end of each action area is a section called "Notes for the Coach" which reviews the above points and offers specific ideas relevant for that chapter.

Note – If your EcoTeam does not include all the members of each household, be sure to encourage each household representative to fully explain each month's program to the rest of his or her household and gain their agreement for any actions undertaken. The household representative will gain a deeper understanding of the program by explaining it, and the success of that household's actions depend critically on a shared commitment and understanding within the household.

5) Close the meeting in a way that celebrates your EcoTeam's accomplishments and commitments to further action. This might be as simple as acknowledging contributions of participants with a "thank-you," or it might be a more elaborate closing reading, music, or ceremony.

Have fun! You and your EcoTeam have at least 6 months of delightful adventure ahead of you, and more if you choose.

Reporting to GAP

In the week following your next monthly EcoTeam meeting, send a completed copy of the "Coach's Report" (at the end of the chapter) to your GAP Coordination Office.

Your GAP Coordination Office is there to support you. It may be regionally based, it may be associated with an organization you belong to, or it may be the national office. You should turn to the people there with your questions and your suggestions, and when you need materials from GAP (such as more workbooks).

The address of your GAP Coordination Office can be obtained from the GAP National Coordination Office, 84 Yerry Hill Road, Woodstock, NY 12498, USA; Phone: 914/679-4830, FAX: 914/679-4834.

Our EcoTeam:
Names & Dates

Use this page to fill in the who, when and where of your EcoTeam. See item 8 on page 8 for more details. Make sure that everyone has a copy of this information.

Name	Address	Phone

Meeting Topic	Coach	Date	Time	Location
Garbage				
Water				
Home Energy				
Transportation				
Eco-wise Consumption				
Empowering Others				

Guidelines for Living in Right Relationship to the Earth

One of the best descriptions of how to live in right relationship with our Earth was a speech delivered by Chief Seattle in his native Duwamish at a tribal assembly in the Pacific Northwest in 1854. We encourage you to consider his words as the spirit in which you do the different actions of the EcoTeam Workbook. Ultimately, it is this spirit that must be breathed into our environmental actions over the next decade to create a sustainable long-term relationship with our Earth.

The Great Chief in Washington sends word that he wishes to buy our land.

Every part of this earth is sacred to my people. Every shining pine needle, every sandy shore, every mist in the dark woods, every clearing, and every humming insect is holy in the memory and experience of my people.

The Great Chief also sends us words of friendship and good will. This is kind of him, since we know he has little need of our friendship in return.

But we will consider your offer. For we know that if we do not sell, the white man may come with guns and take our land.

How can you buy or sell the sky – the warmth of the land? The idea is strange to us.

Yet we do not own the freshness of the air and the sparkle of the water, how can you buy them from us?

Every part of this earth is sacred to my people. Every shining pine needle, every sandy shore, every mist in the dark woods, every clearing, and every humming insect is holy in the memory and experience of my people. The sap which courses through the trees carries the memories of the red man.

The white man's dead forget the country of their birth when they go to walk with the stars. Our dead never forget this beautiful earth, for it is the mother of the red man. We are part of the earth and it is part of us.
The perfumed flowers
are our sisters;
the deer, horse, the great eagle,
these are our brothers.
The rocky crests,
the juices of the meadows,
the body heat of the pony, and man –
all belong to the same family.

So when the Great White Chief in Washington sends word that he wishes to buy our land, he asks much of us.

The great Chief sends word he will reserve us a place so that we can live comfortably to ourselves. He will be our father and we will be his children.

So we will consider your offer to buy our land. But it will not be easy.

The shining water that moves in the streams and rivers is not just water but the blood of our ancestors. If we sell you our land, you must remember that it is sacred, and you must teach your children that it is sacred and that every ghostly reflection in the clear water of the lakes tells of events and memories in the life of my people. The water's murmur is the voice of my father's father.

The rivers are our brothers, they quench our thirst. The rivers carry our canoes, and feed our children. If we sell you our land, you must remember, and teach your children, that the rivers are our brothers – and yours, and you must henceforth give the rivers the kindness you would give your brother.

The red man has always retreated before the advancing white man, as the mist of the mountains runs before the morning sun. But the ashes of our fathers are sacred. Their graves are holy ground, and so these hills, these trees, this portion of the earth is consecrated to us. We know that the white man does not understand our ways. One portion of land is the same to him as the next, for he is a stranger who comes in the night and takes from the land whatever he needs. The earth is not

The perfumed flowers are our sisters; the deer, horse, the great eagle, these are our brothers.

his brother, but his enemy, and when he has conquered it, he moves on. He leaves his fathers' graves behind, and he does not care. He kidnaps the earth from his children, he does not care. His fathers' graves and his children's birthright are forgotten. He treats his mother, the earth, and his brother, the sky, as things to be bought, plundered, sold like sheep or bright beads. His appetite will devour the earth and leave behind only a desert.

I do not know. Our ways are different from your ways. The sight of your cities pains the eyes of the red man. But perhaps it is because the red man is a savage and does not understand.

There is no quiet place in the white man's cities. No place to hear the unfurling of leaves in the spring or the rustle of insect's wings. But perhaps it is because I am a savage and do not understand. The clatter only seems to insult the ears. And what is there to life if a man cannot hear the lovely cry of the whippoorwill or the arguments of the frogs upon a pond at night? I am a red man and do not understand. The Indian prefers the soft sound of the wind darting over the face of a pond, and the smell of the wind itself, cleansed by midday rain or scented with piñon pine.

The air is precious to the red man, for all things share the same breath – the beasts, the trees, the man, they all share the same breath. The white man does not seem to notice the air he breathes. Like a man dying for many days, he is numb to the stench. But if we sell you our land, you must remember that the air is precious to us, that the air shares its spirit with all the life it supports. The wind that gave our grandfather his first breath also receives his last sigh. And if we sell you our land, you must keep it apart and sacred, as a place where even the white man can go to taste the wind that is sweetened by the meadow's flowers.

So we will consider your offer to buy the land. If we decide to accept, I will make one condition: The white man must treat the beasts of this land as his brothers.

I am a savage and I do not understand any other way. I have seen a thousand rotting buffalos on the prairie, left by the white man who shot them from a passing train. I am a savage and I do not understand how the smoking iron horse can be more important than the buffalo that we kill only to stay alive.

What is man without the beasts? If all the beasts were gone, men would die from a great loneliness of spirit. For whatever happens to the beasts soon happens to the man. All things are connected.

You must teach your children that the ground beneath their feet is the ashes of our grandfathers. So that they will respect the land, tell your children that the earth is rich with the lives of our kin. Teach your children what we have taught our children, that the earth is our mother. If men spit upon the ground, they spit upon themselves.

This we know. The earth does not belong to man; man belongs to the earth. This we know. All things are connected like the blood which unites one family. All things are connected.

What is man without the beasts? If all the beasts were gone, men would die from a great loneliness of spirit.

Whatever befalls the earth befalls the sons and daughters of the earth. Man does not weave the web of life, he is merely a strand in it. Whatever he does to the web, he does to himself.

But we will consider your offer to go to the reservation you have for my people. We will live apart in peace. It matters little where we spend the rest of our days. Our children have seen their fathers humbled in defeat. Our warriors have felt shame, and after defeat they turn their days in idleness and contaminate their bodies with sweet foods and strong drink. It matters little where we spend the rest of our days. They are not many. A few more hours, a few more winters, and none of the children of the great tribes that once lived on this earth or that roam now in small bands in the woods will be left to mourn the graves of the people once as powerful and hopeful as yours. But why should I mourn the passing of my people? Tribes are made of men, nothing more. Men come and go, like the waves of the sea.

Even the white man, whose God walks and talks with him as friend to friend, cannot be exempt from the common destiny. We may be brothers after all; we shall see. One thing we know, which the white man may one day discover – our God is the same God. You may think now that you own Him as you wish to own our land, but you cannot. He is the God of man and His compassion is equal for the red man and the white. This earth is precious to Him and to harm the earth is to heap contempt on its Creator. The whites too shall pass – perhaps sooner than all other tribes.

But in your perishing you will shine brightly, fired by the strength of the God who brought you to this land and for some special purpose gave you dominion over this land and the red man. That destiny is a mystery for us, for we do not under-

One thing we know. Our God is the same God. This earth is precious to Him. Even the white man cannot be exempt from the common destiny. We may be brothers after all. We shall see.

stand when the buffalo are slaughtered, the wild horses are tamed, the secret corners of the forest heavy with the scent of many men and the view of the ripe hills blotted by talking wires.

Where is the thicket? Gone. Where is the eagle? Gone. And what is it to say good-bye to the swift pony and the hunt? The end of living and the beginning of survival.

So we will consider your offer to buy our land. If we agree, it will be to secure the reservation you have promised. There, perhaps, we may live out our brief days as we wish. When the last red man has vanished from this earth, and his memory is only a shadow of a cloud moving across the prairie, those shores and forests will still hold the spirits of my people. For they love the earth as the newborn loves its mother's heartbeat. So if we sell you our land, love it as we've loved it. Care for it as we've cared for it. Hold in your mind the memory of the land as it is when you take it. And with all your strength, with all your mind, with all your heart, preserve it for your children and love it – as God loves us all.

One thing we know. Our God is the same God. This earth is precious to Him. Even the white man cannot be exempt from the common destiny. We may be brothers after all. We shall see.

Household Environmental Action Areas

In this section:

Month 1: Reducing Your Garbage

Itinerary for the month:

Month 1: Reducing Your Garbage

How this chapter works

This action chapter, like the five others after it, uses the following sub-sections to help you get the most out of the EcoTeam Program.

Garbage & You: The big picture for the month, it provides you with *background* on why this action is important, *guidelines* for how to approach it, and your *goals* with the reasoning behind them.

This Month's Action Plan: A week-by-week plan that guides you through the month – the heart of the program!

Action Opportunities: A menu of specific actions that you can take to reach your goals.

Worksheet 1: Know Your Garbage: A tool for assessing your garbage output before and after the actions you will take this month.

Notes for the Coach: Suggestions and guidelines for this month's coach.

Coach's Report: The record of your EcoTeam results this month that will be fed back to GAP.

Read all of these before your monthly meeting to orient yourself and then use each as a tool.

Garbage & You

Why garbage is important

Call it waste, call it garbage, call it trash, however you look at it, everything we throw away costs us and the environment both coming and going.

Everything we throw away had to be produced in the first place. That production used up raw materials and energy from the environment, and likely left a trail of pollution along the way – that's the first price.

Throwing it away exacts a second price. At a bare minimum it fills up precious landfill space. (If landfills keep filling up and closing at the rate they have during the 1980s, the U.S. won't have any left by 1995!) But it is not just space. The stew we call garbage usually contains enough toxic materials to pose a major threat of water pollution, and air pollution if it is burned.

Simply put, we have a mess on our

hands. Nevertheless, the crisis of the vanishing landfill could be a blessing in disguise if it forces our throw-away society to rediscover the virtues of reduction, reuse and recycling. Your actions this month can help with that rediscovery.

Increasing our reduction, reuse and recycling of materials can make a major contribution to meeting Earth Day's global environmental goals. For example, using recycled rather than new raw materials typically provides a 50% energy saving and an 85% reduction in industrial air pollution, so it is significant for the global goal of preserving the atmosphere.

The recycling of paper could reduce the demand for virgin wood pulp by 40% and so contribute to the goal of preserving biological diversity.

Finally, using recycled rather than new raw materials typically saves 50% in industrial water use and reduces industrial water pollution by 75% thereby contributing to the global goal of using water wisely.

However you look at it, kicking the throw-away habit will be a big boost for the environment.

Earth Day's Agenda for the Green Decade has two waste-related goals of

Guidelines
- Reduce your intake
- Reuse
- Recycle
- Replace toxic products with non-toxics
- Treat remaining toxics with care.

Your goals
- Get your systems in place to bring your production and handling of waste into environmental balance
- Reduce your garbage by at least 25% by the end of the month
- Reduce your garbage by at least 75% by the end of the decade
- Reduce your hazardous waste by at least 80% by the end of the decade.

direct importance for the household: reducing solid waste by 75% and reducing hazardous waste by 80% by the year 2000. Using the action strategies in this chapter it should be easy to reduce the weight of your garbage that goes to the landfill by at least 25% this month. You may even find that you can reach the 75% goal in this month also!

These action strategies will also enable you to greatly reduce your contribution to hazardous waste.

In absolute terms, each American throws away about 1000 lbs per year or 20 lbs per week. *Your goal is to get down below 5 lbs per person per week by the end of the decade.*

In the U.S. we throw out enough aluminum cans *every three months* to rebuild our entire commercial air fleet.

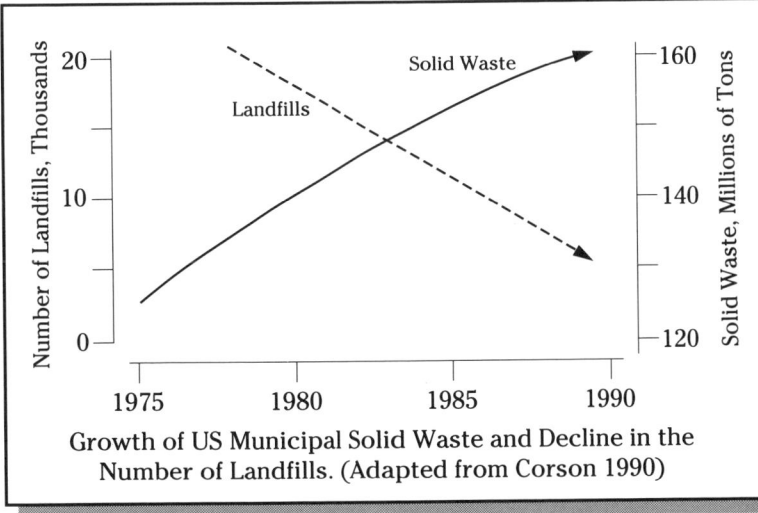

Growth of US Municipal Solid Waste and Decline in the Number of Landfills. (Adapted from Corson 1990)

This Month's Action Plan

Coach's phone number

_____

1st week check-in date and time

_____

Done ☐

2nd week check-in date and time

_____

Done ☐

3rd week check-in date and time

_____

Done ☐

1st week

Use the worksheet "Know Your Garbage" on page 26 to establish how much solid waste of all kinds your household currently produces. At the end of the week check-in, tell your coach what you have found.

2nd week

Use the "Action Opportunities" checklist to look for ways you could reduce your output of solid waste and hazardous waste, and pick the opportunities you want to pursue. At the end of the week check-in, tell your coach:

- what actions you have completed on your own before this program
- what actions you will do this month.

3rd and 4th weeks

Do it! Complete the action steps that you have selected for this month. At the end of the 3rd week check-in, tell the coach what you are working on.

During the 4th week use the worksheet "Know Your Garbage" on page 26 to find out how much you have reduced your garbage this month. Transfer any uncompleted actions you want to do before the end of the program to the "Carry-Over Actions" chart on page 100. All your completed actions will be collected at the end of the program.

Read over the next chapter, "Month 2: Water," in preparation for your next Eco-Team monthly meeting.

At the next meeting tell this month's coach which specific "Action steps for this month" you have completed.

Notes

Every ton of paper made from recycled materials saves about seventeen trees.

Succeeding with your action plan

Our experience with the first EcoTeams has shown that the four week process outlined on the previous page is a great help in enabling you to achieve your goals. To support your success in the program, we suggest the following guidelines.

Do your weekly check-in. This provides *very* important feedback and support within the team, and has proven *essential* for sustaining the motivation for you and for the team.

Be flexible. Within the basic rhythm there *is* room for flexibility. For example, some actions (like avoiding products with excessive packaging) can be done as soon as you see the opportunity (in the 2nd week). Other more complicated actions (like composting) may require more than a month to complete. Use your common sense and follow these guidelines:

- Don't hold back; getting ahead of the rhythm is generally just fine.
- Avoid falling behind by at least getting started on all the actions you intend to complete.

Complete the month's activities. By the end of the month:

- Be ready to let the coach know at the next meeting which "Action steps for this month" you have completed.
- Transfer any uncompleted actions to the "Carry-Over Actions" chart on page 100.
- Find out the results of your actions by using the worksheet to reassess your household garbage output.
- Read over the next chapter, "Month 2: Water," in preparation for your next EcoTeam monthly meeting.

Using the Action Opportunities

The list of actions that begins on the next page gives you specific steps you can take to reduce your garbage output and to do your part in achieving the Earth Day "Agenda for the Green Decade" goals. While these are not the only steps you could take, they are the ones most likely to be both achievable and cost effective.

Treat this list of action opportunities like a menu. Consider every suggested action and then choose from the list those actions that:

- best fit your situation
- will add up to enough garbage reduction to meet your goal.

The list follows a format that is used throughout the program. Please note in particular:

For self-awareness and planning: Next to each *general* action opportunity there is a place to indicate if you have already accomplished this action before the program ("Done before" or "I am doing"), if you intend to do it as part of the program ("I will do"), or if you feel it is not applicable to your situation. If the action is something that can be partially done (for example, you already separate 2 recyclables and now you will increase that to 4), there is space to indicate the appropriate *quantity* of "I am doing" and "More I will do." Fill in whatever is most helpful for planning your actions. This information does *not* get fed back to GAP.

For results: At the end of each general action there is a *specific* "Action step for this month." Use the check box and line to indicate which steps you have completed (now or before) and when. Report which ones you have done to the coach at the end of the month.

A test of 100 households in East Hampton, NY, in 1987 demonstrated that Americans can easily recycle over 80% of their waste!

Your monthly feedback to GAP is based on each "Action step for this month" that you complete during the month (or had previously completed). Reporting these action steps is an essential part of the GAP program.

Notes

Action Opportunities

Learn the 3 R's – Reduce, Reuse, and Recycle

◆ *Think before you buy garbage.*

% I am doing ___

% more I will do ___

(Base these percentages on your own quick estimates of how thoroughly you and your household are doing this action.)

To have less garbage going *out* of your household, begin by bringing less garbage *in*. Packaging and disposable items (like disposable diapers, razors, and plates) make up over 1/3 of the garbage that goes to landfills, so they are prime targets for any garbage reduction campaign. Remember, you pay for all that packaging even though it becomes garbage in less than a week.

Try to avoid excessive packaging of any kind and especially try to avoid packaging that you can't recycle. Paper, glass and metal are generally better than plastics, although many types of plastics are now recyclable as well. Composites of two or more materials (such as gum wrappers of paper and metal foil or "bubble packs" of plastic and cardboard) generally can't be recycled.

Action step for this month: Encourage all the members of your household to think about packaging and discuss the types of packaging to avoid. Agree in your household on what disposable items to avoid.

Action step done ☐

Date _____

(Take credit here for actions done either this month or previously.) ◆

◆ *Think before you throw it away.*

Lots of things that come into your household, like paper bags and envelopes, can be used more than once.

% I am doing ___

% more I will do ___

Action step for this month: Discuss with your household ways to reuse items that you now throw away. Set up easy-to-get-at storage places for anything you intend to regularly reuse, like plastic bags and glass jars.

Action step done ☐

Date _____

(For each action step, tell your coach if you do it this month or did it previously.) ◆

◆ *Separate your recyclables.*

Contact your local recycling center to find out the divisions they use. A workable household system separates:

Nature has no garbage, it recycles everything.
Sooner or later we will need to learn to do the same.

- newspapers
- magazines
- cardboard
- mixed paper
- metal
- glass
- recyclable plastics (mostly jugs and bottles)
- clothing and other "Goodwill" items
- organic waste from the kitchen and yard
- non-recyclable garbage (mostly composites).

Action step for this month: Create, in your house, a designated collection point for each one of these categories (or similar ones that match your local recycling center) and start recycling as much as you can. Even if you have no easy way to recycle all of these items, do this separation for at least a month just to demonstrate to your household how little true garbage you produce.

◆ *Compost.*

Organic waste from your kitchen and yard can be converted into rich fertile soil through a process called composting. Collect your vegetable scraps in a plastic container by your sink, and take them out to your compost pile every few days. What was a problem (garbage) becomes a resource (fertilizer). A good how-to brochure, "Home Composting," is available for $3.00 from Seattle Tilth Association; 4649 Sunnyside Ave N; Seattle, WA 98103. If you don't want to do your own com-

Let It Rot

Almost 18 percent of our garbage is made up of yard wastes, and close to 8 percent is food. You can keep most of it out of our landfills by building a simple compost heap.

1. Twigs 2. Leaves
3. Vegetable, kitchen waste
4. Soil & leaves

Categories I am now
doing   ____#
Categories more I
will do   ____#

Action step done ☐
Date _____
(Actions you complete after this month can be reported at the end of the program.) ◆

I am doing   ☐
I will do   ☐
by (date) _____
Not applicable   ☐

Notes

Notes

posting, often friends who garden are happy to get your organic waste. Many cities also now have municipal composting programs.

> **Action step for this month:** Find a way to return your organic waste to the land, not the landfill.

Action step done ☐

Date _____ ◆

Handle household toxics with care

◆ *Replace the toxics.*

% I am doing ___

% more I will do ___

by (date) _____

A surprising number of ordinary household products, from oven cleaners to permanent press fabrics, contain dangerous chemicals. The good news is that there are many non-toxic alternatives to these products, but you have to know what to avoid and what will work as a replacement. Here is a start:

Frequently toxic product type	Non-toxic replacement product type
Deodorant	Baking soda
Hair Color	Henna
Toothpaste	Baking soda and salt
Drain Cleaner	Baking soda or salt followed by boiling water
All-Purpose Cleaner	Borax, soap, lemon and water
Dishwasher Detergent	Sodium hexametaphosphate
Laundry Detergent	Soap, borax, and baking soda
Glass Cleaners	1/2 vinegar, 1/2 water
Oven Cleaner	Liquid soap, borax, and water
Fabric Softeners	Not needed with natural fabrics
Mold & Mildew Cleaners	Borax, vinegar, and water
Permanent-ink markers	Water-based markers

If you would like to dig deeper into this topic we recommend that you get one of the following:

♦ *Nontoxic, Natural & Earthwise*, by Debra Lynn Dadd, $12.95, Los Angeles: Jeremy P. Tarcher, Inc., 1990.

♦ *The Guide to Hazardous Products Around the Home*, $8.00 from The Household Hazardous Waste Project; Box 87; 901 South National Ave.; Springfield, MO 65804.

If you pour oil, paint or other toxics down the drain, storm sewer or on the ground, it will pollute your groundwater.

◆ "Making the Switch: Alternatives to Using Toxic Chemicals in the Home," $6.00 from Publications Dept.; Local Government Commission; 909 12th St., Suite 205; Sacramento, CA 95814.

Action step for this month: Look through your house to assess your household toxics and replace at least one that you find. Shift your buying habits from toxic to nontoxic items.

Action step done ☐

Date _____◆

◆ *Dispose of them carefully.*

% I am doing ___

% more I will do ___

Many hazardous materials (such as paints, batteries, and oil) don't have easy replacements. Unfortunately many people unthinkingly dispose of these by pouring them down the drain, down a storm sewer, or on the ground. That doesn't get rid of these toxics, rather it pours them, sooner or later, into our water supplies. For example, it is estimated that 40% of the pollution in our waterways comes from the more than 300 million gallons of used motor oil that gets dumped into the environment each year. That is *27 times* more oil *each year* than the Exxon Valdez spill in Prince William Sound, Alaska!

The correct way to handle these items is to either recycle them or have them disposed as hazardous waste. Your local recycling center should know where to take any of these items.

Action step for this month: Find out where you can dispose of hazardous items that are still part of your normal life, like paints, batteries, oil and others. Develop a plan for ongoing proper disposal.

Action step done ☐

Date _____◆

Worksheet 1: Know Your Garbage

The purpose of this worksheet is to help you determine how much solid waste of all kinds your household produces. For one week, separate all your garbage into the following categories (see "Separate your recyclables" on page 23 under "Action Opportunities").

Garbage at the start (lbs per week)

All waste	For the landfill	
_____	_____	◆ newspapers
_____	_____	◆ magazines
_____	_____	◆ cardboard
_____	_____	◆ mixed paper
_____	_____	◆ metal
_____	_____	◆ glass
_____	_____	◆ batteries & toxics
_____	_____	◆ recyclable plastics
_____	_____	◆ clothing and other "Goodwill" items
_____	_____	◆ organic waste from the kitchen and yard
_____	_____	◆ non-recyclable garbage
[ ]	[ ]	Total solid waste in a week

At the end of the week, weigh each group with a bathroom scale. (Borrow one, or something similar, if you don't have one. If you can't get a scale, just estimate as best you can). Put the *full* weight of each pile in the first column. For the second column, put *only* the weight of those items you have been sending to the landfill. Don't include what you are already recycling. For example, if you are recycling your newspapers put their weight in the "All waste" column only. Total each column and then transfer your total starting "landfill" figure (lbs per household per week) to "Before and After Results" on page 98. (If this is an unusual week for garbage, adjust your result to compensate.)

For your own information, divide the total figure for each column by the number of members of your household to get your garbage per person per week. The US average is about 20 lbs per person per week.

Notes

Throwing It All Away

We generate three pounds of garbage per person, per day. Here's what we throw out.

- 17.9% Yard Wastes
- 41% Paper & Paper Board
- 8.7% Metals
- 8.2% Glass
- 7.9% Food
- 6.5% Plastics
- 5.5% Rubber, Leather
- 2.5% Wood, Fabric
- 1.8% Other

These worksheets can give you the gift of knowing that you are personally making a difference.

Next, consider the weight of only the *non-recyclable* garbage (the bottommost line in the chart). This is how low your garbage could be, making no other changes than just separating and recycling. Divide that figure by the number of members of your household and compare that to the Earth Day goal of 5 lbs per person per week. You can bring your non-recyclable garbage down even further by using the Action Opportunities in this chapter.

At the end of the week check-in, tell the coach how much the total "landfill" garbage per week is for your household (total of the second column).

Weigh your total "landfill" garbage again in the 4th week of this month to discover your progress. If you reduce your garbage output further before the last meeting in this program, weigh your total "landfill" garbage yet again to provide a before and after comparison. (We're guessing that you will enjoy this weighing so much that you will be *delighted* to do it three times!)

When you have run your final test, transfer your "after" result for total "landfill" garbage per week for your household to "Worksheet 6: Before and After Results" on page 98.

Garbage example (lbs per week for a household of four)

All waste	For the landfill	
6		◆ newspapers
10	10	◆ magazines
10	10	◆ cardboard
6	6	◆ mixed paper
7	4	◆ metal
7		◆ glass
0.5	0.5	◆ batteries & other toxics
2	2	◆ recyclable plastics
7		◆ clothing and other "Goodwill" items
21	21	◆ organic waste from the kitchen and yard
3.5	3.5	◆ non-recyclable garbage
80	**57**	Total solid waste in a week

Why all this measuring and calculating?

We know from the experience of the first EcoTeams that it is wonderfully empowering to see that *your* actions, taken as part of this program, are actually making a difference.

To have this experience, however, you need to have a reasonably accurate assessment of where you were before the program and where you have gotten to after it.

The worksheets in this chapter and in the others that follow are designed to give you the right balance of accuracy and ease of use. Through them you will be able to:

◆ get an insightful understanding of your household's environmental impact and its potential to improve

◆ contribute to the results GAP is collecting to measure progress towards the global environmental goals.

If you have any difficulty completing these worksheets, get help from your teammates.

Notes for the Coach

Before the monthly meeting

1) Read over this chapter of the workbook carefully.

2) If your EcoTeam is not yet registered with GAP, contact your GAP Coordination Office, or if you don't know where that is, contact the GAP National Office at the address listed on page 145. You need to register to be part of the feedback process and have your actions counted.

3) Prepare for the monthly meeting. It will be very helpful to your team to find out as much as possible about local options for recycling before the meeting.

In the monthly meeting

1) If this is the first meeting, follow the plan under "Initial Meeting" in the introduction to this workbook on page 7 for the first part of the meeting.

2) Review with the group the "Action Opportunities" for this chapter of the workbook.

3) Do a demonstration. One possibility is separating recyclables. (Come prepared with examples for every category you want to use.) Use shopping bags or similar containers to set up collection points for each type of recyclable plus one for true garbage. Use your examples plus the garbage from the house where you are meeting to illustrate what should go into each container.

4) Go over the section "This Month's Action Plan" and make sure everyone understands what to do during the month. Make it clear that at the end of the month you will need to know for your "Coach's Report" which specific "Action steps for this month" (described at the end of each Action Opportunity) each household has completed.

5) Ask who feels they will need help and who would be willing to help. Some team members may anticipate difficulty with part of the process, for example understanding the worksheet or doing some of the actions. Make sure, for each potential area of difficulty, that everyone feels supported with all the help they need. (Some teams have found it helpful to create a "buddy" system for this purpose.)

6) Invite each of your team members to make a clear commitment, for themselves and for the team, to do this month's action plan.

7) Set up logistics for the weekly check-ins using page 20. Each team member should report progress to the coach on a designated day each week. The coach should compile all of the reports (however you want – there is no form in the workbook for this) and call each member of the EcoTeam to give them the compiled report.

8) Close with a sense of mutual celebration and support.

At the end of the month

Use the "Coach's Report" to send your GAP Coordination Office a summary of which specific "Action steps for this month" (described at the end of each Action Opportunity) have been taken and by how many households.

> *"All difficult things have their origin in that which is easy, and great things in that which is small."*
>
> **– Lao-Tsu**

Coach's Report

Please mail or fax a copy of this report to your GAP Coordination Office.

EcoTeam Registration Number: _____

Monthly Coach: _____

Address: _____

_____

Phone: _____

Date: _____   Number of Households in the team: _____

	Number of households that completed this action step:	
This Month's Action Step:	**Previously**	**This month**
Agreed on packaging and disposables to avoid (p. 22)	_____	_____
Set up storage for reusables (p. 22)	_____	_____
Set up separation system for recyclables (p. 23)	_____	_____
Found a way to return compost to the land (p. 24)	_____	_____
Replaced at least one household toxic (p. 25)	_____	_____
Found where to properly dispose of toxics (p. 25)	_____	_____

Use "Previously" *only* when the action was done in the past and no new action was taken this month. Otherwise, all completed actions get counted under "This month."

Carry over actions completed after this month can be reported at the end of the program.

Use a separate sheet to pass on any of the following:

- *personal anecdotes about insights, difficult challenges and their resolution, if applicable*
- *resources or ideas you develop, as well as interesting ways of holding meetings and creative ways of communicating the basic information*
- *feedback on the workbook.*

Thank you for your participation!

Why are we collecting this detailed information?

- Because, through this feedback, your actions motivate others to take action.
- Because your results, communicated through GAP, help people in key parts of the society – media, business, government, etc. – see, in specific detail, the ability of direct and positive grassroots action to achieve the global goals.
- Because your experience helps us learn how the program can be improved and serve others better.

This feedback is an essential part of the EcoTeam Program. We appreciate your taking the time to make the program work.

Month 2: Improving Home Water Efficiency

Itinerary for the month:

Month 2: Improving Home Water Efficiency

Water & You

Why home water use is important

The good news about water is that there is enough of this renewable resource so that everyone could have an ample supply of clean fresh water if we were to use it as efficiently and carefully as present day technologies permit.

The bad news, of course, is that we don't. All over the world supplies of fresh water are being squeezed between 1) growing demand from agriculture, industry, and households and 2) growing pollution that makes existing supplies less and less usable.

Even in places where the water supply still seems adequate, extensive water use causes lots of environmental problems. Great amounts of energy are used to transport, heat and treat water, so wasting water also wastes energy. Diverting water from rivers and lakes destroys natural habitats and may interfere with the

Our bodies are more than 75% water.

migration of fish, preventing them from reproducing. It also destroys recreational opportunities. Waste water dumped back into rivers and lakes is similarly damaging.

Water that comes from underground aquifers is often being used faster than it is replenished. We have grown dependent on "fossil water" in a way that is as unsustainable as our dependence on fossil fuels. Not only will the aquifers run out at some point, but cave-ins in the emptying aquifers damage the aquifers in ways that cannot be repaired.

At a more personal level, reduced water use can lead either to lower water and sewer bills or, if you have a well, to lower utility bills since electricity is required to pump the water. In areas with poor drainage, reduced water use can save you from septic tank and drain field overflow.

Even though households account for only 7.5% of water use in the US (agriculture is the big user, accounting for

Water is the blood of life. The oceans, the rivers, the clouds, and our bodies are a single bloodstream.

over 80%), households account for 57% of publicly supplied water. The high water quality required for household use means that supply systems and disposal systems are more complicated, expensive and energy intensive, and available sources are more restricted.

Equally importantly, the household is where society's fundamental habits are expressed and formed. If we use water wisely in our households, we will have the awareness and commitment to make sure water is used wisely in agriculture and industry as well.

Guidelines

◆ Develop water saving habits

◆ Fix leaks

◆ Buy the most water efficient fixtures and appliances.

Your goals

◆ Get your systems in place to bring your home water use into environmental balance

◆ Reduce your water use by at least 10% by the end of the month

◆ Reduce your water use by at least 30% by the end of six months.

(If you are in a drought area you may want to set higher goals.)

The Earth Day goal for home water use is a 30% reduction by the year 2000. It turns out that this is so easy for most people to achieve that we are suggesting you do it during the next six months. You may well find you can do it all this month!

In absolute terms, average household per person water use in the US is about 150 gallons per day, with about 80 gallons for indoor use and 70 gallons for yard watering and other outdoor uses.

Your goal is to get your household's per person water use down below 100 gallons per day.

Because there is so much variation in outdoor use – from location to location and season to season – we will track indoor and outdoor separately in this chapter. Using this month's program you will be able to find out just how much water your household is using. If your water use is greatly different from the average you may want to adjust this goal according to your circumstances (see the worksheet "Assessing Your Water Use" on page 42 in this chapter for suggestions.)

You could live only about a week without water.

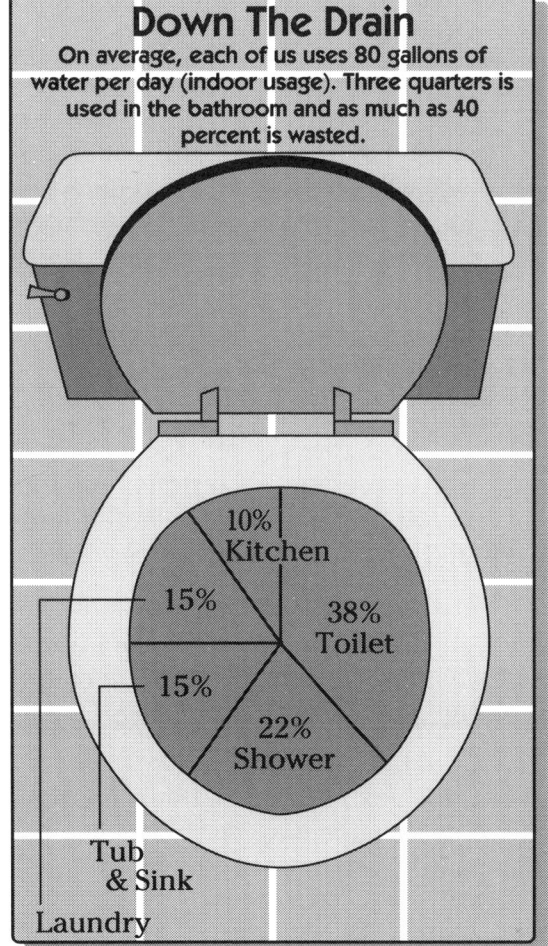

Down The Drain

On average, each of us uses 80 gallons of water per day (indoor usage). Three quarters is used in the bathroom and as much as 40 percent is wasted.

10% Kitchen

15%

15%

38% Toilet

22% Shower

Tub & Sink

Laundry

Remember to do your weekly check-in, be flexible, and complete the month's activities.

This Month's Action Plan

_____

1st week
check-in date
and time

_____

Done ☐

2nd week
check-in date
and time

_____

Done ☐

3rd week
check-in date
and time

_____

Done ☐

For guidelines
on succeeding
with your
action plan,
see page 21 in
Month 1.

1st week

Use the worksheet "Assessing Your Water Use" on page 42 to establish how much water your household is currently using. At the end of the week check-in, tell your coach how much water per person per year your household uses.

2nd week

Use the "Action Opportunities" checklist to look for ways you could save water, and pick the opportunities you want to pursue. At the end of the week check-in, tell your coach which actions you've checked as "done before/am doing" and which you "will do."

3rd week

Gather the products, help, and equipment you will need to take the actions you have chosen for this month. For example, if you plan to upgrade your shower heads, purchase them this week. At the end of the week check-in, tell the coach what you are now prepared to do.

4th week

Do it! Complete the action steps for this month that you have selected and prepared for during the previous weeks.

Read over the next chapter, "Month 3: Energy," in preparation for the next Eco-Team monthly meeting. Transfer any uncompleted actions to the "Carry-Over Actions" chart on page 100.

At the next meeting tell this month's coach which specific "Action steps for this month" you have completed.

Notes

Action Opportunities

This section gives you specific steps you can take to help bring your home water use into environmental balance and to do your part in achieving the Earth Day "Agenda for the Green Decade" goals. While these are not the only steps you could take to improve your home water efficiency, they are the ones most likely to be both achievable and cost effective. Some of these actions cost money, but they will generally pay for themselves in less than 3 years thanks to both water and energy savings. They are like stock that pays you more than 33% dividends!

You will, of course, have to adjust these actions to your own living situation. If you are renting a house or an apartment, some of the major actions (like installing a low-flow toilet) may not apply to you – but don't rule yourself out too quickly. Many of the actions (like replacing your shower head) pay for themselves in a year or less.

Treat this list of action opportunities like a menu. Consider every suggested action and then choose from the list those actions that:

- best fit your situation
- will add up to enough water savings to meet your goal.

If you have already accomplished some of these steps before the start of this program, congratulations! Be sure to take credit in the check boxes and "savings estimators" that follow for what you have already done toward meeting your goal.

Use the checklists at the start of each action opportunity for awareness and planning.

Use the checklists at the end of each action opportunity, by the "action step," for your reportable results (see page 21 in Month 1).

Changing fixtures indoors

Most plumbing fixtures (toilets, faucets, shower heads, etc.) were not designed for efficient water use, so you can often make major savings by simply switching to better designed fixtures. Here are some things you can do:

◆ *Install toilet dams or plastic jugs.*

Put toilet dams, plastic bottles filled with water, or some similar water displacer in your toilet tank to reduce the amount of water used with each flush. (Don't use bricks unless you put them in plastic bags since the grit from them can harm the toilet. If you use plastic bottles, weight them with a few stones to keep them from moving around and interfering with

Notes

Number of toilets
done before _____

Number more
I will do _____

by (date) _____

Not applicable ☐

Notes

the flushing mechanism.) Since the toilet is the biggest water user in the house, this simple action can save a lot of water – typically enough to reach your 10% goal in one single step!

> **Action step for this month:** Install some water reducer in your toilets.

Action step done ☐

Date _____◆

◆ *Install water-saving shower heads.*

There are now many new high-performance designs that give you an invigorating spray with up to 75% less water use. Since showers are usually more than 50% hot water, this will also save a lot of energy, so you will get credit for this action next month as well as now. This double savings can pay for the cost of these shower heads in as little as two months! If you get one with a convenient on/off control you can save even more water by turning off the water while you soap-up (see "Wet-down,..." on page 40).

> **Action step for this month:** Install water-saving shower heads.

Number of showers done before ____

Number more I will do ____

by (date) _____

Not applicable ☐

Action step done ☐

Date _____◆

◆ *Install water-saving faucet aerators.*

Like the low-flow shower heads, these sophisticated designs for your kitchen and bathroom sinks break up the water into lots of drops – more effective for washing and rinsing. Most have an on/off control that allows additional savings.

> **Action step for this month:** Install water-saving faucet aerators.

Number of faucets done before ____

Number more I will do ____

by (date) _____

Not applicable ☐

Action step done ☐

Date _____◆

◆ *Replace your toilets with the new ultra-low-flow designs.*

These toilets require less than 1.5 gallons per flush. Replacing your toilet might sound like a big step, but San Diego and several other cities have found that it is cheaper to give homeowners a $100 rebate for each toilet they replace than it is to expand their city water system. If you are in a dry area, building a new house, own your own well, have problems with your septic system, or need to replace any toilet, this is an action worth considering.

Number of toilets done before ____

Number more I will do ____

by (date) _____

Not applicable ☐

The washing power of water depends on surface area, not volume, so droplets are more efficient than streams.

Action steps for this month: Find the local suppliers of low-flow toilets. Find out whether or not your local water department gives rebates for installing these toilets. If they don't, ask why not.

Action step done ☐
Date _____ ◆

◆ *When you get a washing machine or dishwasher, check for water (and energy) efficiency.*

Done before ☐
Will do ☐
Not applicable ☐

Front loading clothes washers can save up to 1/3 of water use. The more efficient models of other appliances can get similar savings, and since these generally use hot water, this means energy savings as well.

Action step for this month: Find out about water-saving appliances and where you can buy them, and share your findings with your teammates at the next meeting. Plan to use this research next time you get a new water-using appliance.

Action step done ☐
Date _____ ◆

◆ *Fix leaks.*

Done before ☐
Will do ☐
by (date) _____
Not applicable ☐

Even small leaks in toilets or dripping out of faucets can waste thousands of gallons of water a year. You can check for leaks in a toilet by putting dye in the toilet tank and then seeing if it seeps into the bowl. Most household leaks are easily fixed by replacing worn parts. Hardware and plumbing stores carry what you need. Since there is no such thing as a "typical" leak, we can't estimate how much water you will save. Nevertheless, if you have leaks they can easily waste more water than you use on everything else!

Action step for this month: Check all your faucets and toilets for leaks and fix any you find.

Action step done ☐
Date _____ ◆

Notes

Using the savings estimator

The "savings estimator" is a tool that can help you decide which actions will be most effective in reaching your goals.

The estimator lists each action opportunity together with estimates for the typical savings you can expect to get by fully implementing each action. These percentages are given relative to the particular category of water use (such as toilet, shower, etc.) and relative to total home water use.

For example, installing toilet dams can save about 1/3 of the water use by toilets. Since toilets account for about 38% of all home water use, the 1/3 savings in the toilet category translates into a 12% overall savings for the home.

If you fix leaks this month, make your own estimate for how much water that will save.

The procedure for using the estimator is as follows:

- For actions that you have either completely "done before" 100% or "will do" completely, simply copy the value from the "% of Indoor Total" column into the appropriate "done before" or "will do" column. For example, if you will install low-flow shower heads in all your showers, copy 16% into the "will do" column.

- For actions that you have either "done before" or "will do" only partially, you need to reduce your estimated savings. For example, if you have two toilets, one already has plastic jugs in it, and you plan to put jugs in the other one, split the 12% into 6% in the "done before" column and 6% in the "will do" column.

You can get a rough estimate of your total savings by adding up the estimated percent savings in the "done before" and "will do" columns. For example, if you have "Install toilet dams" and "Install water-saving shower heads" under "will do" you would add 11% to 16% and then put 27% under the "will do" column.

If you have some "done before" items, congratulations! Take credit for these towards meeting your goals. If you have a lot of "done before" items you may want to set higher goals for your household since the benefits from these savings don't stop at the minimum goals we are using in the program. It would be great if you would also share your experience in these actions with your teammates.

Note that this is only a rough estimate based on typical housing conditions. Your actual savings may be significantly different. But at least these estimates will enable you to set your own priorities.

Remember, your overall goals for home water savings are 10% this month and 30% in 6 months. These savings will come from not only the "fixtures" actions in this estimator but also from the "habits" actions later in this section.

Finally, use this estimator as a place to keep track of when you have completed each action that you listed in the "will do" column.

Notice that you could exceed the goal of a 30% reduction with just the first three actions!

Reducing your shower and faucet use by 75% will typically save 10% of home energy costs. Add this in next month.

If you need help, ask your coach or other teammates. That's part of the fun of being on a team!

Saving hot water, from the shower and tap, could save about 10% of your home energy costs.

Estimator 1. Water savings from efficient fixtures.

Action for Indoor Fixtures	Typical Savings – % of:		Estimated Savings		Completion Date
	Category	Indoor Total	Done Before	Will Do	
Install toilet dams or plastic jugs	33	12	_____	_____	_____
Install water-saving shower heads	75	16	_____	_____	_____
Install water-saving faucet aerators	60	7	_____	_____	_____
Install ultra-low-flow toilet	80	30	_____	_____	_____
Switch to water-efficient appliances	33	5	_____	_____	_____
Fix leaks	?	?	_____	_____	_____
Estimated Indoor Fixtures Savings (% of Indoor Total)[a]:			_____	_____	

[a] **For the technically minded**: Strictly speaking the "% savings" figures shouldn't be added. Rather, each saving should be converted to a use-rate by subtracting the % savings from 100 and then dividing by 100. These use-rates should then be multiplied to produce an overall use-rate. Finally, an overall savings rate can be obtained by subtracting the overall use-rate from 1 and multiplying by 100. For example, a 2% savings translates into $(100 - 2) \div 100 = .98$ for the use rate. A 2% and an 8% savings produce an overall use rate of $.98 \times .92 = .9016$ and that implies an overall savings of $1 - .9016 = .0984$ or 9.84% (or approximately 10%). The approximation of addition gets worse as the savings get larger and as more items of savings are included. However, the rough quality of the initial estimates hardly justifies the complexity of the more accurate method.

Changing habits

A little extra thoughtfulness, backed up by good fixtures, can save even more water. If you have an ample water supply, your household may not want to make full use of all of the conservation strategies listed here. We recommend, however, that you at least try them out. Remember that the enthusiasm in your household for making these changes will depend a lot on how they are presented. Be sure to mention all the reasons for saving water described under "Background" at the beginning of this section. The habit changes that last are the ones that are freely chosen. Here's what you can do:

◆ *Be mindful with the tap.*

Whether you are brushing your teeth, shaving, or washing dishes, turn the water on only when you need it. Be sure to get the kind of faucet aerator that has an on/off switch to make it easy to temporarily shut the water off without having to adjust the temperature. You can save 75% or more of your tap use this way.

Notes

% I am doing ____

% more I will do ____

(Base these percentages on your own quick estimates of your household's behavior.)

Combining new fixtures with new habits, you can easily save more than 50% of your current water use.

Action step for this month: Show all the members of your household how to save water this way and then do it.

Action step done ☐

Date _____ ◆

◆ *Wet-down, soap-up, rinse-off.*

% I am doing ___

% more I will do ___

When you shower, turn off the water while you soap-up. Again, be sure to get a shower head with an on/off switch so that you don't have to adjust the temperature. You can save 75% and more of your shower use this way, plus similar energy savings.

Action step for this month: Describe this technique to all the members of your household. Experiment to find a comfortable way – that maintains or enhances your showering enjoyment – to make this part of your showering habits.

Action step done ☐

Date _____ ◆

◆ *Flush less.*

% I am doing ___

% more I will do ___

Small amounts of urine hardly need to be flushed every time.

Action step for this month: Agree within your household on guidelines for when to flush.

Action step done ☐

Date _____ ◆

Estimator 2. Water savings from indoor habits.

Action for Indoor Habits	Typical Savings – % of:		Estimated Savings		Completion Date
	Category	Indoor Total	Done Before	Will Do	
Be mindful with the tap	75	9	_____	_____	_____
Wet-down, soap-up, rinse-off	75	16	_____	_____	_____
Flush less	50	19	_____	_____	_____
Estimated Habit Savings (% of Indoor Total)[a]:			_____	_____	
Combined Estimated Indoor Savings (Add results from Estimators 1 and 2)[a]:			_____	_____	

[a] See footnote a, Estimator 1, page 39.

Many people use more water for their lawns than for all their indoor uses.

Outdoor Actions

◆ *Conserve on yard watering.*

% I am doing ___
% more I will do ___
Not applicable ☐

Lawn watering and other outdoor water uses account for almost half of all home water use. If you water your yard or garden, do it during the coolest part of the day to avoid evaporation. Local conditions will determine whether morning or evening is best.

Action step for this month: Agree within your household on guidelines for when and how much to water your yard and garden.

Action step done ☐
Date _____◆

◆ *Be mindful with the hose.*

% I am doing ___
% more I will do ___
Not applicable ☐

If you use a garden hose for washing the car or similar uses, don't let it just run. A nozzle with an easy on/off switch makes it easier.

Action step for this month: Install an on/off nozzle on your hose. Show all the members of your household how to use it to save water.

Action step done ☐
Date _____◆

◆ *Xeriscape.*

Done before ☐
Will do ☐
Not applicable ☐

This unusual word refers to the practice of landscaping with plants, often natives, that don't require much water. The result is often more beauty and less work than conventional landscaping.

Action step for this month: Find a local source for low-water demand plants and more information about xeriscaping.

Action step done ☐
Date _____◆

Notes

Estimator 3. Water savings from outdoor actions

Action for Outdoor Actions	Typical Savings – % of:		Estimated Savings		Completion Date
	Category	Outdoor Total	Done Before	Will Do	
Conserve on yard watering	40	38	_____	_____	_____
Be mindful with the hose	75	3	_____	_____	_____
Xeriscape	50	48	_____	_____	_____
Estimated Outdoor Savings (% of Outdoor Total)[a]:			_____	_____	

[a] See footnote a, Estimator 1, page 39.

In many localities, saving water will save you money on your water bill.

Worksheet 2: Assessing Your Water Use

Reuse this worksheet just before your team's last meeting to calculate your average daily "after" usage.

Here is an example of how this works:

Suppose you get records for the past year...

And then you get 3 months more after this month ...

Say your past year total = 200,000 gal...
200,000÷365 = 548 gal/day.

Say your new 3 month total = 34,200 gal...
34,200÷90 = 380 gal/day.

Or, say your past usage for the 3 months = 45,000...
548 x (34,200÷ 45,000) = 416 gal/day.

Your goal, in the first week of this month, is to find out your year-round average daily water usage in gallons per day. If you have a water meter, check your past water bills, or ask your water company/city water department to give you their figures on your water use. The ideal is to have a full year's month-by-month history. This will give you the most accurate results and allow you to distinguish between indoor use (fairly steady year round) and outdoor use (heaviest in the warm season, frequently zero in the winter).

If you can get a good history of your water use, fill in the following monthly usage chart. Put the name of the most recent month at the right end of the top row and then work back to the left. Put the corresponding gallons/month in the past use row. Fill in the corresponding new use over the coming months. Use the worksheet below to calculate your "before" and "after" average daily usage.

Monthly Water Usage Chart

Month												
Past use												
New use												

(Note: To convert to gallons from cubic feet or ccf, 1 cubic foot of water = 7.5 gallons; 1 ccf = 750 gallons.)

"Before" calculation:

Total past usage = sum of monthly usage = _____ gallons over _____ days.

Average daily "before" usage = total past usage ÷ number of days = _____ gal/day.
Transfer this result to "Before and After Results" on page 98.

"After" calculation if your past water use was fairly constant over the year:

Total new usage = sum of new monthly usage = _____ gallons over _____ days.

Average daily "after" usage = total new usage ÷ number of days = _____ gal/day.
Transfer this result to "Before and After Results" on page 98.

"After" calculation if your past water use varies with the seasons:

Total new usage = sum of new monthly usage = _____ gal.

Corresponding past usage (over the same months as new usage) = _____ gal.

Average daily "after" usage = (average daily "before" usage) times

(total new usage ÷ corresponding past usage) = _____ gal/day.
Transfer this result to "Before and After Results" on page 98.

Everywhere, saving hot water saves you money on your energy bill.

If you don't have a water meter, you will have to estimate your water use. Put a sheet of paper next to every toilet, shower and tub in your house. On these sheets keep count for a week of each toilet flush, each bath, and the length of each shower. At the end of the week, calculate your overall usage as follows:

number of flushes in a week times 5 gallons per flush = _____

number of baths times 36 gallons per bath = _____

total minutes of showers times 5 gallons per minute = _____

sub-total = _____

times 1.3 (to get indoor total) = _____ gal/week

times 1.8 (more or less, to get outdoor total) = _____ gal/week

divided by 7 = _____ gal/day

Add up your figures for flushes, baths and showers, then multiply that total by 1.3 to account for all the other indoor uses (like the washing machine). The result will be a rough estimate for your weekly indoor household use.

Since average outdoor use is almost the same as average indoor use, you should double (more or less, depending on your outdoor use) the above estimate to get your household weekly total. To get your daily use, divide the weekly household use by 7.

If you want to get more accurate figures for your shower usage, you can time how long it takes to fill a one gallon plastic jug with the shower going at your normal rate. If it fills in 10 seconds, that's 6 gallons a minute, 20 seconds is 3 gallons a minute, and so on.

Whatever method you have used, transfer your "Before" result to "Before and After Results" on page 98.

Figuring your "After" result

If you have metered water, keep track of your new water use over the next few months to give a before and after comparison. Just before your team's last meeting, use the worksheet on the previous page to calculate your average daily "after"

usage. If your past usage was fairly constant throughout the year, use the first method. If not, use the second. Transfer your result to "Before and After Results" on page 98.

If you don't have metered water, plan to rerun the one week tally on your water use before your team's last meeting. A good time to do it is as soon as you have finished all the water-saving actions you plan as part of the program.

Be sure to use lower figures for gallons per flush (say, 3) and gallons per minute on the shower (say, 2) if you have modified these fixtures to reduce their water use. Transfer your "After" result to "Before and After Results" on page 98.

To determine your *per person* water use, divide your daily household use by the number of people in your household.

The average U.S. household water use is about 150 gallons per person per day. If your use is quite different from the U.S. average, you may want to adjust your goals. You can either use the 30% reduction goal or you can use the absolute goal of 100 gallons per person per day and figure a new percentage goal. In any case, if you feel you have a valid reason for choosing a non-average goal, do it.

Here is how this one works:

Say that in the week your household had 100 flushes, 4 baths, and 60 minutes of showers.

100 x 5 = 500
4 x 36 = 144
60 x 5 = <u>300</u>
subtotal = 944

944 x 1.3 = 1227 gal/week

1227 x 1.8 = 2209 gal/week

2209 ÷ 7 = 316 gal/day

That's all there is to it.

"Those who cannot tell what they desire or expect still sigh and struggle with indefinite thoughts and vast wishes"
—Emerson

Notes for the Coach

Before the monthly meeting

1) Read over this chapter of the workbook carefully.

2) Prepare for the monthly meeting. Read over the section on "Facilitating an EcoTeam Meeting" in the introduction on page 8 for general guidelines and suggestions.

In the monthly meeting

1) Open the meeting in a way that provides insight into this month's theme.

2) Check-in on experiences and results from the previous month.

3) Review with the group the "Action Opportunities" for this chapter of the workbook.

4) Do a house tour – looking for places to save water. This tour provides a practical demonstration of the situations described in the "Action Opportunities." (Prepare for this on your own before the meeting, then during the meeting lead the group to what you found.) Go through the house where the meeting is being held. Look at some or all of:

- opportunities for behavior changes that can save water
- the toilet (Is it the normal 5 gallon or more type? Is there anything in the water tank to reduce water use?)
- the shower and taps (Are they low-flow types? Is it easy to turn the water on and off without changing the temperature?)
- the garden hose (Does it have an easy on/off nozzle?).

5) Go over the section "This Month's Action Plan" and make sure everyone understands what to do during the month. Make it clear that at the end of the month you will need to know which specific "Action steps for this month" each household has completed.

6) Ask who feels they will need help and who would be willing to help. Some team members may anticipate difficulty with part of the process, for example doing the calculations for the worksheet or some of the physical actions involved in changing equipment. Make sure, for each potential area of difficulty, that everyone feels supported with all the help they need. (Some teams have found it helpful to create a "buddy" system for this purpose.)

7) Invite each of your team members to make a clear commitment, for themselves and for the team, to do this month's action plan.

8) Set up logistics for the weekly check-ins on page 34. Each team member should report progress to the coach on a designated day each week. The coach should compile all of the reports and call each member of the EcoTeam to give them the compiled report.

9) Close with a sense of mutual celebration and support.

At the end of the month

Use the "Coach's Report" to send the GAP Coordination Office a summary of which specific "Action steps for this month" (described at the end of each Action Opportunity) have been taken and by how many households.

"A jug fills drop by drop" – Gautama Buddha

Coach's Report

Please mail or fax a copy of this report to your GAP Coordination Office.

EcoTeam Registration Number: _____

Monthly Coach: _____

Address: _____

_____

Phone: _____

Date: _____   Number of Households in the team: _____

This Month's Action Step:	Number of households that completed this action step:	
	Previously	This month
Installed toilet dams or plastic jugs (p. 36)	_____	_____
Installed water-saving shower heads (p. 36)	_____	_____
Installed water-saving faucet aerators (p. 36)	_____	_____
Found supplier of ultra-low-flow toilets (p. 37)	_____	_____
Researched water-saving appliances (p. 37)	_____	_____
Checked for and fixed leaks (p. 37)	_____	_____
Showed household about conserving tap use (p. 40)	_____	_____
Showed household about conserving shower use (p. 40)	_____	_____
Agreed on when to flush (p. 40)	_____	_____
Agreed on when and how much to water the yard (p. 41)	_____	_____
Installed on/off nozzle on the hose (p. 41)	_____	_____
Found out about xeriscaping (p. 41)	_____	_____

Use "Previously" *only* when the action was done in the past and no new action was taken this month. Otherwise, all completed actions get counted under "This month."

Carry over actions completed after this month can be reported at the end of the program.

Use a separate sheet to pass on any of the following:
- *personal anecdotes about insights, difficult challenges and their resolution if applicable*
- *resources or ideas you develop, as well as interesting ways of holding meetings and creative ways of communicating the basic information*
- *feedback on the workbook.*

By providing this feedback, you are helping to inspire and motivate others and improve the EcoTeam Program. Thanks for taking the time to make the program work.

Month 3: Improving Home Energy Efficiency

Month 3: Improving Home Energy Efficiency

Energy & You

Why home energy use is important

Most of the energy we use to heat our homes and power our appliances comes from the burning of fossil fuels. The burning of these fuels in turn is one of the major sources of acid rain and CO_2 (carbon dioxide), a major contributor to the greenhouse effect.

Home energy use accounts for about 17% of all energy use in the US. It is responsible for 3.95 tons of CO_2 per person per year and 15 lbs of acid rain producing SO_2 and NO_x. Less energy use means less CO_2 and other pollutants get spewed out into the air. Thus improvements in home energy efficiency are directly connected to the global goal of preserving the climate and atmosphere.

Fortunately, there is much you can do through energy efficiency to get *more* comfort and benefit from your energy use while using less – often *considerably* less.

According to Rocky Mountain Institute, we in the US could save, by using today's cost-effective energy-efficient technologies, about *75%* of our energy use with no loss of comfort or benefit!

Guidelines

- Develop energy saving habits
- Plug your energy leaks by insulating and weatherstripping
- Buy the most energy-efficient appliances and lighting
- Use good architectural and landscape design to get the most out of passive solar heating, summer shade, and natural ventilation.

Your goals

- Get your systems in place to bring environmental balance into your home energy use
- Reduce your home energy use by at least 5% by the end of the month
- Reduce your home energy use by at least 10% by the end of six months
- Reduce your home energy use by at least 30% by the end the decade.

With this month's actions you could save more than $100 each year for *every* person in your household!

The Earth Day goal for home energy use is a 30% reduction by the year 2000, enough to head us onto a sustainable path. There are easy steps you can take right away to reduce your energy use by at least 5%, and other steps you will take during the next few months as part of this program will further reduce your energy use.

Achieving the 30% reduction goal will save, on average, about 1 ton of CO_2 per person per year. That ton is as much as the CO_2 that gets absorbed in a year by 5.4 trees or that gets released by burning 100 gallons of oil. At $1.00 per gallon, achieving your 30% reduction thus represents a typical yearly savings for your household of $100 per person. At higher oil prices, the savings are even greater.

Using this month's program you will be able to find out just how much CO_2 your household is generating. If your energy use now is greatly different from the average, you may want to adjust your goals according to your circumstances. (See the worksheet "Reading Your CO_2 Meter" on page 64 for suggestions.)

In any case, since saving energy generally also means saving money, there is really no reason to stop improving your energy efficiency just because you have reached one of these goals. This is characteristic of almost all of the actions recommended in this program. They are win-win benefits, not compromises. By doing them you will help the environment, improve your own quality of life and save – all at the same time.

Getting your hands dirty

Some of the actions for this month require construction work or changes in equipment. If you are handy with tools or can get help from other members or your EcoTeam or your family, you'll be able to do much of this work yourself. But be careful – remember safety is important!

If you want to contract for some or all of the construction work, ask other Eco-Team members or friends to recommend contractors or use the Yellow Pages to identify possible contractors. Get two or three quotes for the work and make sure you understand just what the contractor proposes to do. Then check out their references and select the contractor you most trust to do the work well and at a fair price.

Of course, this applies only to construction and equipment changes. Changing your habits is up to you!

If you were to use all of the action opportunities in this chapter, you could easily save more than 75% of your household energy consumption.

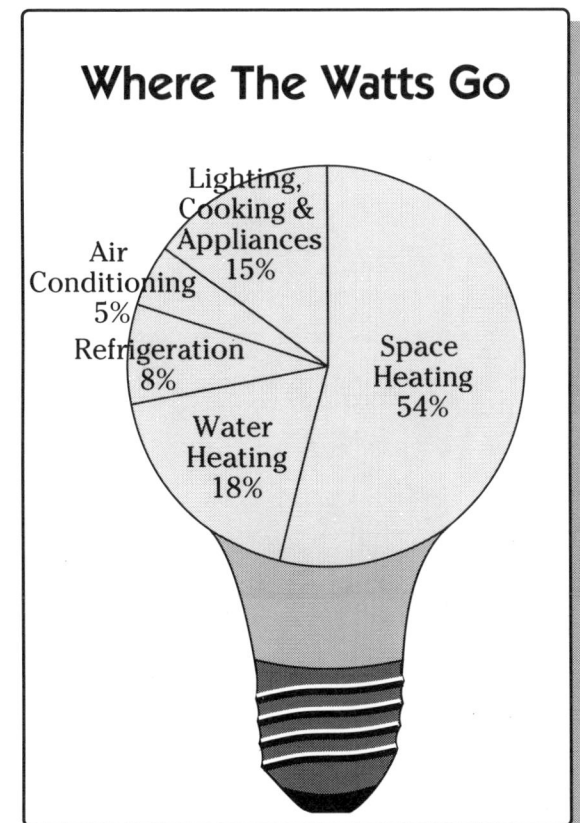

Where The Watts Go

Lighting, Cooking & Appliances 15%

Air Conditioning 5%

Refrigeration 8%

Water Heating 18%

Space Heating 54%

Any carry-over actions from previous months that you have completed can be reported at the end of the program.

This Month's Action Plan

Coach's phone number

Notes

1st week
check-in date
and time

Done ☐

1st week

Use the worksheet "Reading Your CO_2 Meter" to establish how much energy your household is currently using. At the end of the week check-in, tell the coach how much CO_2 per person per year your household generates.

2nd week
check-in date
and time

Done ☐

2nd week

Use the "Action Opportunities" checklist to look for ways you could save energy, and pick the opportunities you want to pursue. At the end of the week check-in, tell your coach which actions you've checked as "done before/am doing" and which you "will do."

3rd week
check-in date
and time

Done ☐

3rd week

Gather the products, help, and equipment you will need to take the actions you have chosen for this month. For example, if you will do weatherstripping, purchase supplies this week. At the end of the week check-in, tell the coach what you are now prepared to do.

4th week

Do it! Complete the action steps for this month that you have selected and prepared for during the previous weeks.

Read over the next chapter, "Month 4: Transportation," in preparation for the next EcoTeam monthly meeting. Transfer any uncompleted actions to the "Carry-Over Actions" chart on page 102.

At the next meeting tell this month's coach which specific "Action steps for this month" you have completed.

For guidelines on succeeding with your action plan, see page 21 in Month 1.

Renters can often do more to save energy than most people imagine.

Action plan supplement for renters and condominium owners

To decide if you need this supplement, begin by determining which of the following four descriptions best fits your relationship with your housing:

- Your household owns a single family dwelling ("house-owner")
- Your household rents a single family dwelling ("house-renter")
- Your household owns a condominium in a multi-household building ("apartment-owner")
- Your household rents an apartment in a multi-household building ("apartment-renter")

The rest of the material in this chapter can be used without modification by house-owners. This supplement provides suggestions and modifications for the other three housing relationships.

The basic difference between these other three groups and house-owners is that as a renter or apartment-owner you may want and/or need the cooperation of others outside your household – your landlord, building superintendent, and/or other households in your apartment building – for some of the suggested actions in this chapter.

This need for cooperation with your "larger household" can have many positive results for you such as:

- creating win-win-win actions
- experiencing a stronger sense of community
- experiencing the satisfaction that can come from shared action.

Let's look at these more closely. Perhaps the most important thing to realize about actions that require this cooperation is that all of these actions have benefits for everyone. They are truly win-win-win actions (a win for you, for the others, and for the Earth). Thus they provide you with the opportunity to work with these other people with a quality of shared community that you may have never experienced before.

The last month of the program, "Empowering Others," asks everyone in the program to look at how we can help others take environmentally responsible action. You get to start sooner on this because in this month, dealing with "Home Energy," you will likely need to involve the members of your "larger household." Thus you will have the opportunity to more fully experience the sense of community that can be one of the powerful benefits of participating in the EcoTeam Program.

Guidelines

- Think positive. There are many creative ways for renters and condominium owners to cooperate with their "larger household" to bring it into environmental balance.
- Identify all the potential benefits for each person – neighbors and landlord.
- Be willing to spend time researching the possibilities and educating others.
- Proceed on the basis that the actions you want done are in everyone's interest.
- Be creative in developing arrangements that are fair in sharing both costs and benefits with everyone.

An example will help to clarify these guidelines. One of the action opportunities this month is "plug the air leaks" (see page 56), that is, plugging the leaks of hot

In 1987 the 90.5 million US households were distributed among the housing types as follows: 62% house-owners, 11% house-renters, 3% apartment-owners, and 24% apartment-renters.

air out and cold air in through cracks, especially around windows and doors. If we look at the costs and the benefits of this action we can begin to see why everyone can win through cooperating.

Plugging air leaks by weatherstripping around windows and doors has immediate costs, both in money and in time.

Balancing these costs are lots of benefits, all based on the fact that it now takes less energy to keep your household warm. Therefore:

- there is less pollution from energy production going into the environment
- money is saved through lower utility bills, often paying for the cost of the weatherstripping in a year or less
- the household is more comfortable because it is less drafty
- the value of the property is increased.

Obviously, a house-owner can get all these benefits, but what happens to the others? Let's look back at the list of benefits:

- Obviously, we all – renters, landlords and homeowners alike – benefit from less pollution.
- If you don't pay the utility bill, or don't plan to stay long, the money saved this way won't be much of a direct benefit to you. However, it will be a benefit to the landlord, so you can use this saving as an argument to get the landlord to support this action (see examples on page 54).
- As a renter you get full benefit from the greater comfort in the house.
- As a renter you get no benefit from the

improved property value, but again you can use this as an argument for the landlord.

The net result is that everybody gets some benefit, but these benefits are split. It makes sense then that the costs should also be split – and this requires cooperation between you and your landlord.

There are many ways to divide the "costs." What is fair will depend on the particular situation. However, when you think about these costs, don't think only in terms of money. Time and effort are important also. In many situations landlords will be willing to pay a major part of the dollar costs if tenants will provide the time and effort. In other situations it may be appropriate to divide both the effort and the dollar cost more evenly.

The rest of this supplement provides suggestions for developing an action plan for this month that will enable you to fully develop the opportunities in *your* situation

1st Week

Your exact course of action this week will depend on your particular housing situation. However you do it, your goal is to 1) gain clear information about your past energy use, and 2) begin to inform and involve your landlord, building superintendent and/or neighbors.

If you are renting and don't pay part or all of the utilities, you will need the cooperation of your landlord and/or others to get the information on past energy use for the worksheet "Reading Your CO_2 Meter." Thus as part of assessing your situation this week, you will need to inform others about the EcoTeam Program and determine their willingness to support your efforts.

It might help to explain to them that

There are many ways to divide the "costs." What is fair will depend on the particular situation.

Consider your whole building as your larger household.

you are involved in an international environmental program designed to help people bring their households into environmental balance. You are interested in information about past energy use in your building to help you identify actions that could save both energy and money. Make it clear that these actions will be in everyone's interest, and that you are willing to do your part to bring them about.

If you are in an apartment building and some or all of the energy is not individually metered, you won't be able to separate your use from your neighbors' use. You can, nevertheless, use overall values of energy use for the building to provide a basis for estimating your household's energy use. Just divide the total building energy use by the number of households in the building and then use that average energy use per household for your own energy use.

In addition, you may well choose to take actions that will affect the whole building. For that purpose you will want to know the total building energy use.

By the way, if you live in an apartment you are likely to find that your heating energy use is relatively low – both because apartments tend to be smaller than houses and because apartments have less surface area (walls and roof) exposed to the outside. You many even find that you have already achieved the goals for this month. Even if you have, however, there are many good reasons to still take action for even lower energy use. Many apartment buildings, even with these advantages, are much less energy-efficient than they could be.

2nd Week

We suggest you use the list of "Action Opportunities" to look for ways you could save energy, and pick the opportunities you want to pursue. You may want to do this with others in your larger household, or do it on your own. At the end of the week check-in, tell your coach which actions you've checked as "done before/am doing" and which you "will do."

We recognize that as a renter or a condominium owner you may have less chance to take some of the actions suggested in the workbook. For example, you can't turn down your thermostat if you don't have one!

The key to getting full benefit from this month's action opportunities is to look for things you *can* do, and to consider your whole building to be your larger household. Because all of the suggested actions are good investments that pay for themselves quickly, benefit the environment, and generally improve comfort, they are strongly win-win-win. Chances are good that you can get cooperation from others, especially if you provide leadership in identifying what could be done and how.

One of the best opportunities in old apartment buildings with central heating involves improving the controls and the insulation for the heating system, both at the furnace and throughout the building. Modern controls can be much more efficient than the old systems, and they often pay for themselves in under two years. Central domestic hot water heating systems (which often use the same furnace) offer a similar opportunity for improvement.

If you do have your own thermostat, but don't pay the utility bill, you might want to see if your landlord would be willing to reduce your rent based on the amount of energy you save. An example of this is provided by a woman in Vermont who owns two rental apartment build-

> Households in buildings with 5 or more units used an average of only 56% as much energy as households in single family dwellings.

In one case, adding extra insulation provided an unexpected bonus. It saved both the renters and the landlord a great deal of cost and headache by preventing the house and its water pipes from freezing during an extended power outage.

ings. As the landlord, she pays the electric bill, so she has an interest in keeping energy use down. To encourage this, she has an arrangement with her renters where she refunds to them (deducts off their rent) the full amount that any renter saves in electricity below the average usage for the past three years. She (and other landlords like her) would probably be delighted to have renters suggest energy efficiency improvements.

Many of the bigger actions can also be accomplished in a rental situation. An example of this comes from Washington State. A family renting an old house that was built without any insulation in the walls was able to convince their landlord to have insulation blown into the walls. The arrangement they used to split the costs goes like this:

♦ The renters did all the research and made all the arrangements.

♦ The renters provided the cash to pay 3/4 of the bill; the other 1/4 was paid by a state government program.

♦ The renters then deducted enough from the rent so that within a year they were repaid in full amount.

Since the renters pay the utility bills, they got the benefits of a more comfortable house and lower bills. The landlord got a more valuable house, and both got a cleaner environment.

As an added bonus, the insulation saved both the renters and the landlord a great deal of cost and headache by preventing the house and its water pipes from freezing. An unusually bad winter storm knocked out power and heat for 4 days of subfreezing weather. When the power and the heat finally came back on, the house was only 2 degrees above freezing! If the walls had not been insulated the pipes would have been frozen long before the power came back.

For further resources for action opportunities, contact your state energy office. Two free booklets you might find useful are:

♦ *Multifamily Housing Energy Conservation Workbook*, New York State Energy Office; 2 Rockefeller Plaza; Albany, NY 12223.

♦ *Making Rental Housing Energy-efficient*, HUD-CPD 1269; US Dept of Housing and Urban Development; Washington, DC 20410.

3rd & 4th Week

Get the support of the others (like your landlord) who need to be involved in any actions you have chosen. Develop an action plan together, including agreement on how costs and effort should be split. Then work together to follow your shared plan.

We are confident that many EcoTeam members who are renters and condominium owners will find wonderfully creative ways to apply the principles of the Household EcoTeam Program to their particular situations. You may make some of these wonderful discoveries yourself. Whatever you discover and invent, please let us know so that we can pass it along!

How is *your* electricity generated?
Coal, nuclear, hydro, gas, oil, wind, sun?

Action Opportunities

This section gives you specific steps you can take to bring your home energy use into balance with the environment and to do your part in achieving the Earth Day "Agenda for the Green Decade" goals. While these are not the only steps you could take to improve your home energy efficiency, they are the ones most likely to be both achievable and cost effective. Some of these actions cost money, but they will generally pay for themselves in less than three years. They are thus investments, and very good ones at that. They are like a bank account that gives you more than 33% interest – forever!

Treat this list of action opportunities like a menu. Consider every suggested action and then choose from the list those actions that:

◆ best fit your situation

◆ will add up to enough energy savings to meet your goal.

If you have already accomplished some of these steps before the start of this program, congratulations! Be sure to take credit in the checklists and calculations that follow for what you have already done toward meeting your goal.

Use the checklists at the start of each action opportunity for awareness and planning.

Use the checklists at the end of each action opportunity, by the "action step," for results you'll report (see page 21 in Month 1).

Home heating and cooling

This is the biggest single energy use in the home, accounting on average for 59% of overall home energy use. Here are some things you can do to save energy, money, and the air around us:

◆ **_Turn the thermostat down on your heating system; turn it up on your cooling system._**

Estimates are that you can save 2% on your heating for every degree you turn your thermostat down.

Action step for this month: Agree within your household on the temperature at which to set the thermostat.

◆ **_Turn down the thermostat at night or when you leave the house._**

This doesn't save as much as a steady turn down, because you will have to warm the space back up later, but the savings can still be substantial. A thermostat with a timer can make this process easy.

Action step for this month: Agree within your

Notes

I am doing ____°F

More I will do ____°F

Not applicable ☐

Action step done ☐

Date _____ ◆

I am doing ____°F

More I will do ____°F

Not applicable ☐

Action step done ☐

Notes

household on the amount to turn down the thermostat at night. Optionally, purchase and install a timed thermostat.

Date _____ ◆

◆ *Tune-up your furnace.*

This involves clean-up and adjustment and can be done by a service person or you can learn to do it yourself. For more information get the booklet "Heating Systems" from: Public Information Office; Massachusetts Audubon Society; Lincoln, MA 01173.

Done before ☐
Will do ☐
by (date) _____
Not applicable ☐

Action step for this month: Make an appointment for a furnace tune-up OR order the booklet so that you can do it yourself.

Action step done ☐
Date _____ ◆

◆ *Plug the air leaks.*

Air leaks, often around windows and doors, are one of the biggest sources of heat loss in most houses. The simplest step you can take is to check, and if necessary add or replace, the weatherstripping around windows and doors. If you want to be more thorough, get a specialist to check the whole house for leaks and then seal them. In one study, careful testing for, and then sealing of, air leaks saved homeowners an average of 30% on their heating bills.

% done before ___
% more I will do ___
by (date) _____
Not applicable ☐

Action step for this month: Weatherstrip around windows and doors OR make an appointment to get your house thoroughly checked and sealed.

Action step done ☐
Date _____ ◆

◆ *Add storm windows and doors.*

These can help with both the air leaks around windows and doors and with the heat that radiates through windows.

% done before ___
% more I will do ___
by (date) _____
Not applicable ☐

Action step for this month: If you have only single-pane windows and single doors, make an appointment for an estimate on adding another layer.

Action step done ☐
Date _____ ◆

◆ *Plant trees to shade your house.*

You can save money on air conditioning and cooling, make your house more pleasant, and do a

Done before ___#
More I will do ___#
by (date) _____

How is your house oriented relative to the sun?
Where is the prevailing wind in the summer, in the winter?

bit for reforestation by planting leafy trees around your house. Position the trees on the west and east so that they will provide shade in the summer but let light into the house in winter. In colder climates, trees on the north side of the house can block the wind and keep the house warmer.

Not applicable ☐

> **Action step for this month:** Contact a local nursery to find out what trees they recommend and the best time for planting. If the season is right, plant the trees. Otherwise, mark that date on your calendar and commit yourself to do it.

Action step done ☐

Date _____ ◆

◆ *Insulate walls and ceilings.*

% done before ___
% more I will do ___
by (date) _____
Not applicable ☐

Older houses often don't meet today's insulation standards, even if they have some insulation. Check with your heating company or utility to find out what your local standards are, and check to see if your house meets them. Uninsulated walls should be filled and attics can often have insulation added. (Money saving tip: Local utilities often have programs that pay for a significant part of the cost of improving your home insulation. They will also often provide free home energy audits. Contact your utility to find out what they offer.)

> **Action step for this month:** If your house is already well insulated, give yourself credit. Otherwise, make an appointment with an insulation contractor to give you an analysis and an estimate on bringing your house up to (or beyond) current standards.

Action step done ☐

Date _____ ◆

◆ *Install passive solar heating.*

% done before ___
% more I will do ___
by (date) _____
Not applicable ☐

Passive solar heating is now a mature and cost-effective technique. In practice it can range all the way from some well-placed southern windows to the elegance of an attached greenhouse or solarium. In fact, you probably already have some passive solar heating even if you don't call it that.

> **Action step for this month:** Make an appointment with an architect or designer who specializes in solar design to give you an estimate of what your solar possibilities are OR

Action step done ☐

Date _____ ◆

Notes

There are now hundreds of buildings in cold climates that are so well designed they need no heating at all!

Notes

get a book on passive solar design and do your own estimate.

Use the following "savings estimator" to help you decide which actions will be most effective in reaching your goals, just as you did last month for your water saving actions (see page 38).

For example, if you are planning to "Tune-up your furnace" and "Weatherstrip windows and doors," take the number 3% for "Tune-up your furnace" in the "Home Total" column and place it in the "Will Do" column, and similarly take the 11% that goes with "Weather-strip windows and doors" and also place it in the "Will Do" column. If you plan to only partially weatherstrip, put in less than 11%, for example 6% for doing only half.

Once you have placed all your estimated percentage savings in the "Done Before" and "Will Do" columns, add these to give a rough subtotal for heating and cooling actions. For the above example, you would add 3% to 11% and then put 14% under the "Will Do" column. Later in the chapter you will combine these estimates with estimates for savings from water heating, appliances and lighting to get an overall home total.

Note that this is only a rough estimate based on typical housing conditions. If you want a more accurate estimate you should get a home energy audit from your utility company or from an energy consultant.

Estimator 4. Energy savings from home heating and cooling actions.

The overall goals for home energy savings are 5% this month; 10% in 6 months; 30% by 2000.

Action for Home Heating & Cooling	Typical Savings – % of:		Estimated Savings		Completion
	Heating	Home Total	Done Before	Will Do	Date
Turn down the heat 3°F	6	3	_____	_____	_____
Install a timed thermostat	5	3	_____	_____	_____
Tune-up your furnace	5	3	_____	_____	_____
Weatherstrip windows and doors	20	11	_____	_____	_____
Add storm windows and doors	30	16	_____	_____	_____
Plant trees to shade house	50[a]	0-6[a]	_____	_____	_____
Insulate walls and ceiling	60	32	_____	_____	_____
Install passive solar heating	75	40	_____	_____	_____
Heating & Cooling Sub-Total (% of Home Total)[b]			_____	_____	

[a] Percent of cooling. The savings estimate will vary greatly with climate and your use of air conditioning.

[b] See footnote a, Estimator 1, page 39.

Where does the oil and gas you use for home energy come from? What are all the steps on its journey to you?

Hot water

This is the second biggest energy use in the home, typically about 18% of overall home energy use. Here are some things you can do to save energy, money, and the atmosphere. (Other actions that save both water and energy were part of the "Water" chapter last month.)

◆ *Turn down the thermostat on your water heater.*

The best setting seems to be 130°F, cool enough to save energy but hot enough to kill bacteria. If you, like many people, had it set at 140°F, the 10°F drop will save 6% of the energy used. If your heater has an "energy conservation" setting, use that.

> **Action step for this month:** Set your water heater's thermostat to 130°F. If that means turning it up from a lower setting, consider it as health insurance.

Done before ___ °F

More I will do ___ °F

by (date) _____

Not applicable ☐

Action step done ☐

Date _____◆

◆ *Insulate your water heater and hot water pipes.*

Special insulating "blankets" are available that easily go over water heaters. You can get them from hardware stores or some utilities provide them. Beyond the heater, hot water pipes can also be insulated. This is especially important for any part of the system in an unheated space, but even in the house uninsulated pipes add to the energy required for summer cooling, as well as wasting hot water energy. Special easy-to-install pipe insulation is available from hardware stores.

> **Action step for this month:** Insulate all of the accessible and uninsulated parts of your hot water system.

% done before ___

% more I will do ___

by (date) _____

Not applicable ☐

Action step done ☐

Date _____◆

◆ *Install a demand water heater.*

Demand water heaters contain no tank – they simply heat water as it is needed. This eliminates heat loss from the tank, saving up to 20-30%. They are not a universal solution, since water quantity is limited to about 3 gallons per minute, and the pilot

Done before ☐

Will do ☐

by (date) _____

Not applicable ☐

Notes

Notes

light on the gas units can sometimes waste more energy than is saved by having no tank. Yet in the right situation, they are great. They work best where hot water demand is small (as in a small household) and/or infrequent (as in a vacation home), or in conjunction with solar or wood stove water heating.

Action step for this month: Research demand water heaters to see if they would save energy in your situation.

Action step done ☐
Date _____ ◆

◆ *Replace an electric water heater with a gas or oil water heater.*

Since most electricity is generated by burning some fossil fuel, heating water with electricity is a relatively inefficient two-step process. In fact, the average gas water heater produces less than 60% of the CO_2 produced in generating the electricity for a comparable electric water heater.

Done before ☐
Will do ☐
by (date) _____
Not applicable ☐

Action step for this month: If you have an electric water heater, contact an appliance dealer to find out what it would cost to switch next time your heater needs to be replaced.

Action step done ☐
Date _____ ◆

◆ *Install a solar water heater or pre-heater.*

In many parts of the country solar hot water heating is cost-effective, and it can easily save 50% or more of the energy you need to purchase. Solar water heating, like all uses of solar energy, is totally renewable and has essentially no adverse environmental impact. Solar energy will be at the heart of our long-term energy future, so why not start now?

Done before ☐
Will do ☐
by (date) _____
Not applicable ☐

Action step for this month: Make an appointment with an installer of solar water heaters for an estimate OR get a book on solar water heaters and do your own estimate.

Action step done ☐
Date _____ ◆

The biggest energy using appliances are refrigerators, clothes dryers, color TVs, stoves, furnace fans, and water-bed heaters.

Estimator 5. Energy savings from home hot water heating actions.

Action for Home Water Heating	Typical Savings – % of:		Estimated Savings		Completion Date
	Hot Water	Home Total	Done Before	Will Do	
Turn water heater down to 130°F	6	1	_____	_____	_____
Insulate water heater and pipes	20	4	_____	_____	_____
Install a demand water heater	20	4	_____	_____	_____
Replace electric with gas or oil	40	7	_____	_____	_____
Install a solar water heater	50	10	_____	_____	_____
Reduce hot water use	50[a]	10[a]	_____	_____	_____
Water Heating Sub-Total (% of Home Total)[b]			_____	_____	

[a] Based on your actions in the previous "water" month.

[b] See footnote a, Estimator 1, page 39.

Appliances

Twenty three percent of home energy use is distributed among various appliances, with refrigerators at the top of the list. Many appliances now come in designs that require only 50% as much energy as standard designs, or less. There are refrigerators that use only 20% as much as conventional models.

◆ *Buy energy-efficient appliances.*

Careful purchasing of appliances could save up to 13% of your total household energy use. An excellent resource for energy-efficient appliances (and just about every action opportunity in this chapter) is the *Consumer Guide to Home Energy Savings: Listings of the Most Efficient Products You Can Buy...and Much More* by Alex Wilson. It is available for $6.95 + $2.00 postage from the publisher, the American Council for an Energy-Efficient Economy; 1001 Connecticut Ave NW, Suite 535; Washington, DC 20036.

> **Action step for this month:** Find out about energy-efficient appliances from this book and/or from dealers. Plan to use what you have learned the next time you need to get a new appliance.

Notes

Done before   ___#

More I will do   ___#

by (date)   _____

Not applicable   ☐

Action step done ☐

Date _____◆

Most small kitchen appliances, stereo equipment, computers, etc. use very little total energy.

◆ *Tune up your refrigerator.*

Refrigerators and freezers on average account for 7.5% of total home energy use, and almost 40% of appliance energy use. After space heating and water heating, they are the single biggest item. To get full value out of the energy your refrigerator is using:

- Locate it away from direct sunlight or heat sources like an oven. Make sure there is a least an inch of clearance so that air can circulate around it.

- Once a year or so, vacuum or brush off the condenser coils (at the back or behind a front grill) to prevent a dust build-up from insulating the coils and making them less efficient.

- Check the door seal. If you can slide a sheet of paper past the seal when the door is shut, you need to replace the seal.

- Adjust the temperature with the help of an accurate thermometer. The refrigerator should between 36 and 38°F, and the freezer between 0 and 5°F.

Action step for this month: Check the condition of your refrigerator, cleaning and adjusting it as necessary.

Done before ☐
Will do ☐
by (date) _____
Not applicable ☐

Action step done ☐
Date _____◆

Lights

Lighting accounts for only about 3% of total energy use, but there are still opportunities for significant savings.

◆ *Install energy-efficient lighting.*

Fluorescent lights use only 25% as much energy for the same light output as incandescent lights. Older fluorescents often had problems with both flicker and color that bothered some people, but today you can get "full-spectrum" fluorescents (they have a color balance similar to sunlight; much better than "daylight" bulbs) and better fixtures. (For top quality, look for fixtures with ballasts rated "energy-saving type B with type A sound.")

Especially easy to use are the recently developed compact fluorescent bulbs that screw into an ordi-

% done before ___
% more I will do ___
by (date) _____
Not applicable ☐

Using all the actions in this chapter you could save over 75% of your energy and still get the same benefits!

nary socket in place of an incandescent bulb and have a similar color. Compact fluorescents cost more initially, but they last 10 times longer and save $30 to $50 in energy costs over their lifetime. Be aware, however, that they are larger than conventional incandescent bulbs and won't fit in all fixtures.

In apartment buildings hallways and common areas are ideal locations to install fluorescents.

Action step for this month: Replace at least one high-use incandescent light in your house with a compact fluorescent.

Notes

Action step done ☐

Date _____ ◆

Estimator 6. Energy savings from efficient appliances and lights.

Action for Appliances and Lights	Typical Savings – % of:		Estimated Savings		Completion
	Category	Home Total	Done Before	Will Do	Date
Buy energy-efficient appliances	50	11	_____	_____	_____
Tune-up your refrigerator	30	2	_____	_____	_____
Install energy-efficient lighting	75	2	_____	_____	_____
Appliances and Lights Sub-Total (% of Home Total)[a]			_____	_____	

[a] See footnote a, Estimator 1, page 39.

Summarize your household energy savings by totalling the savings from the heating and cooling, water-heating, and appliances and lights estimators.

Estimated Savings (% of Total Home Energy Use)	Done Before	Will Do
Estimator 4 (Heating and Cooling):	_____	_____
Estimator 5 (Water Heating):	_____	_____
Estimator 6 (Appliances and Lights):	_____	_____
Total Household Energy Savings (% of Home Total)	_____	_____

This worksheet can provide you with a sound basis for reducing your contribution to global warming.

Worksheet 3: Reading Your CO_2 Meter

If you need help completing this worksheet, ask your coach or other team mates.

This worksheet is designed to enable you to find out how much energy your household is currently using, how much it is costing and how much CO_2 emission your household is currently contributing to global warming.

1) Begin by finding out your household energy use for the past year (or less if you can't get a full year) by one of the following:

♦ looking at past bills
♦ calling your energy company (they usually have detailed records)
♦ getting costs from your check register. You can use a current bill to find out how much each unit of energy costs ($ per kwh, per gallon, or per gas unit) and use this to estimate energy use from your previous payments. (cont. next page)

We have not included wood heat because trees absorb CO_2. As long as wood burning is balanced with planting new trees, wood burning makes no net CO_2 change in the atmosphere.

Most recent month: –>

This month: –>

Example:
6,000 kwh
x 1.5 = 9,000
500 gal
x 22 = 11,000
500 gas units x
12 = 6,000
Total CO_2 =
26,000 lbs.

Household Energy Use: Past History

Month	Electricity		Oil		Gas	
	Cost	Use (kwh)	Cost	Use (gal)	Cost	Use (units*)
Totals:						
CO_2	kwh x 1.5 =		gal x 22 =		unit* x 12 =	

Total Household CO_2 = _____ lbs in _____ months

Total Household Energy Cost = $_____ in _____ months

_____

*Gas is most commonly measured in one of three units: ccf (hundred cubic feet), therms (100,000 BTUs), or gallons (for propane and bottled gas). Even though these are not equivalent units, it turns out that they each have about the same heat content and produce about the same amount of CO_2, so for this worksheet you can use any one of these units interchangeably.

Energy efficiency offers us great potential to improve our quality of life while reducing our environmental impact.

2) Fill in the "past history" chart on the preceding page with the information you have found. Leave one line for *this* month at the bottom, put the most recent month above it, and work up.

3) Total your cost and use for each type of energy.

4) Convert energy use into CO_2 emissions by multiplying kwhs of electricity by 1.5, gallons of fuel oil by 22, and gas units by 12. Add these to get your total household CO_2 emission. The chart below provides an example for October through December.

Household Energy Use: Past History – Example

Month	Electricity Cost	Use (kwh)	Oil Cost	Use (gal)	Gas Cost	Use (units*)
October	$16	200	$80	80	----	---
November	$17	220	---	---	$40	50
December	$20	247	$120	120	----	---
Totals:	$53	667	$200	200	$40	50
CO_2	kwh x 1.5 =	1000	gal x 22 =	4400	unit* x 12 =	600

Total Household CO_2 = __6000__ lbs in __3__ months

Total Household Energy Cost = __$293__ in __3__ months

---

5) Use the following steps to calculate your household CO_2 emission per year and per person per year:

- Divide your [Total Household CO_2] by the number of months you have included in the total (if you have included 9 months of history, divide by 9) to get [Total household lbs of CO_2 per month]. Here's how:

  [Total lbs of CO_2] ÷ [months of history] = [Total household CO_2 per month]

  _____ lbs ÷ _____ months = _____ lbs per month

- Multiply this [Total household CO_2 per month] by 12 to get [Total household CO_2 per year]. Here's how:

  [Total household CO_2 per month] x 12 = [Total household CO_2 per year]

  _____ lbs per month x 12 = _____ lbs per year

  This is your "Before" result. Transfer it to "Before and After Results" on page 98.

- Divide this [Total household CO_2 per year] by the number of people in your household to get [CO_2 per person per year]. Here's how:

  [Total household CO_2 per year] ÷ [number of people in household] = [CO_2 per person per year]

  _____ lbs per year ÷ _____ people = _____ lbs per person per year.

  Report this number to your coach at the end of the week check-in.

Example:

Suppose your household has generated 18,000 lbs of CO_2 in 9 months...

18,000 ÷ 9 = 2,000 lbs per month.

Then 2,000 x 12 = 24,000 lbs per year.

For a 4 person household, 24,000 ÷ 4 = 6,000 lbs per person per year.

To get a good before and after comparison, keep track of your energy use over the coming months.

To find out how much impact the actions you take this month will make, use the table below to record your energy use in the coming months. Begin by putting your cost and use for the first month *after* this month on the top line of the chart, and then fill down for each coming month.

We have given you enough room for a full year's energy use so that, for your own interest, you can get a comparison with last year that includes all seasons. You might want to keep a copy of this worksheet near where you pay bills to make it easy.

Household Energy Use: Future

Month	Electricity		Oil		Gas	
	Cost	Use (kwh)	Cost	Use (gal)	Cost	Use (units*)
Totals:						
CO$_2$	kwh x 1.5 =		gal x 22 =		unit* x 12 =	

First month after: –>
2nd after: –>
3rd after: –>
etc.

Example:

Suppose your new sub-total is 4,000 lbs in the 3 months of February through April.

Suppose last year's corresponding subtotal was 7,000 lbs and your "Before" number was 24,000 lbs per year.

Your "After" number will be: (4,000÷7,000) x 24,000 = 13,714 lbs per year.

New Sub-Total Household CO$_2$ = _____ lbs in _____ months

New Sub-Total Household Energy Cost = $_____ in _____ months

Last Year's Corresponding Household CO$_2$ = _____ lbs in _____ months

Last Year's Corresponding Household Energy Cost = $_____ in _____ months

To get an estimate for your new total household lbs of CO$_2$ per year, divide your number for [New Sub-Total Household CO$_2$] by your number for [Last Year's Corresponding Household CO$_2$] and then multiply the result by your "Before" values for total household CO$_2$ per year from the previous page. Here's how:

[New Sub-Total ÷ Last Year's Corresponding] x ["Before"] = [New per year]

[_____ lbs ÷ _____ lbs] x _____ lbs per year = _____ lbs per year

This is your "After" result. Transfer it to "Before and After Results" on page 98.

We can extend our positive impact by carrying the awareness we have gained in the household into the society around us.

Figuring your "After" result

Just before the last meeting of the six-month program, add up your new costs and energy use for the months *after* you finished this chapter on "Improving Home Energy Efficiency." Convert your new total energy use into CO_2 emission just as you did before and enter your result as "New Sub-Total Household CO_2" on the line provided.

Next, go back to your "past history" chart and add up the costs and energy use for last year's *corresponding* months only. For example, if your new energy use covered the months of February, March and April, include only last February, March and April in your last year's corresponding months sub-total. You need to make this comparison to last year's corresponding months because energy use varies so greatly from season to season. Thus it would not be accurate to compare the few months after the changes with the full year before the changes.

Calculate your new usage using the formulas and examples at the bottom of the preceding page. Transfer your estimated new total to "Before and After Results" on page 98.

Note: If you have done this program during a season of the year that requires very little heating or cooling, you may need to make adjustments to this estimate if you took actions that should affect heating and/or cooling. Use the percentages in the "savings estimators" for the actions you took. For your own interest we suggest you keep track of your energy use for a full year to see how you are doing and how accurate your estimates are.

Customizing your goals

Average US household energy use is responsible for 7900 lbs of CO_2 per person per year.

The Earth Day goal is a 30% reduction in home energy use by the year 2000. Relative to the average, this would mean a goal of 5530 lbs of CO_2 per person per year. However, your situation may not be average. If it isn't, you can either 1) use the 30% reduction figure to set your goal, or 2) choose the absolute value of 5530 lbs of CO_2 per person per year as your goal and figure out a new percentage based on the ratio of your present usage to this goal. There are many reasons why you might legitimately need to choose a goal different from the average. You may live where there are especially cold winters and thus have to use more energy (although superinsulated houses in Canada need little more than lights and appliances to keep them warm all winter!). You may work at home, and thus energy use that would usually be expected at the workplace shows up on your home bill. If you feel you have a valid reason for choosing a non-average goal, do it.

Wood heating

If you want to include the CO_2 production from wood heat, figure that a ton of air-dried wood produces about 3400 lbs of CO_2. Since the density of wood varies greatly with species, this translates to the range of 3500 to 7100 lbs of CO_2 per cord. As a rough estimate, use 4000 lbs of CO_2 per cord for softwoods and 6000 for hardwoods.

If you are heating with wood you can minimize your CO_2 production by burning dry wood, using an efficient stove, and planting trees.

Most scientists agree that doubling the CO_2 in the atmosphere would lead to serious global warming. Each pound of CO_2 released in the atmosphere is enough to double the CO_2 concentration in about 20,000 cubic feet of air, or about the size of a typical suburban house. If your household produced 24,000 lbs of CO_2 in the last year, you can think of this as 24,000 house-fulls of global warming.

> *"What an immense power over the life is the power of possessing distinct aims."* — Elizabeth Stuart Phelps

Notes for the Coach

Before the monthly meeting

1) Read over this chapter of the workbook carefully.

2) Prepare for the monthly meeting. Read over the section on "Facilitating an EcoTeam Meeting" on page 8 for general guidelines.

3) Contact your local utility to find out what resources they offer and be ready to share that information with the EcoTeam. Often utilities can provide information and assistance to help you save energy. Their services may include free materials, services, or household energy use audits. They may also be able to direct you to loans, grants, tax incentives, or rebates to help implement energy saving projects.

In the monthly meeting

1) Open the meeting in a way that provides insight into this month's theme.

2) Check-in on experiences and results from the previous month.

3) Review with the group the "Action Opportunities" for this chapter. Make sure everyone, house-owners, renters and apartment owners, is well supported in understanding how these actions could apply in their situations.

4) Do a house tour – looking for places to save energy. This tour provides a practical demonstration of the situations described in the "Action Opportunities." (Prepare for this on your own before the meeting, then during the meeting lead the group to what you found.) Go through the house where the meeting is being held. Look at some or all of:

- opportunities for behavior changes that can save energy
- the water heater (Is the thermostat set above 130°F? Is it insulated? Are the hot water pipes insulated?)

- the insulation in the walls (Take off an electrical outlet cover to look, carefully, into the wall cavity, or look up in the attic.)
- cracks around windows and doors
- opportunities for improving the performance of the refrigerator
- other action opportunities from this chapter.

5) Go over the section "This Month's Action Plan" and make sure everyone understands what to do during the month. Make it clear that at the end of the month you will need to know which specific "Action steps for this month" each household has completed.

6) Ask who feels they will need help and who would be willing to help. Some team members may anticipate difficulty with doing the calculations for the worksheet or some of the physical actions involved in changing equipment. Make sure, for each potential area of difficulty, that everyone feels supported with the help they need. (Some teams have found it helpful to create a "buddy" system for this purpose.)

7) Invite each of your team members to make a clear commitment, for themselves and for the team, to do this month's action plan.

8) Set up logistics for the weekly check-ins using page 50. Each team member should report progress to the coach on a designated day each week. The coach should compile all of the reports and call each member of the EcoTeam to give them the compiled report.

9) Close with a sense of mutual celebration and support.

At the end of the month

Use the "Coach's Report" to send the GAP Coordination Office a summary of which specific "Action steps for this month" (described at the end of each Action Opportunity) have been taken and by how many households.

"Adopt the pace of nature, her secret is patience."
– Ralph Waldo Emerson

Coach's Report

Please mail or fax a copy of this report to your GAP Coordination Office.

EcoTeam Registration Number: _____

Monthly Coach: _____

Address: _____

_____

Phone: _____

Date: _____   Number of Households in the team: _____

This Month's Action Step:	Number of households that completed this action step:	
	Previously	**This month**
Agreed on daytime thermostat setting (p. 55)	_____	_____
Agreed on nighttime thermostat setting (p. 56)	_____	_____
Began furnace tune-up process (p. 56)	_____	_____
Began plugging air leaks (p. 56)	_____	_____
Got estimate on storm windows and doors (p. 56)	_____	_____
Chose shade trees to plant (p. 57)	_____	_____
Got estimate on upgrading insulation (p. 57)	_____	_____
Assessed passive solar potential (p. 58)	_____	_____
Set water heater to 130°F (p. 59)	_____	_____
Insulated hot water pipes (p. 59)	_____	_____
Researched demand water heaters (p. 60)	_____	_____
Researched replacing electric water heater (p. 60)	_____	_____
Researched solar water heaters (p. 60)	_____	_____
Researched energy-efficient appliances (p. 61)	_____	_____
Cleaned and adjusted refrigerator (p. 62)	_____	_____
Installed at least one energy-efficient light (p. 63)	_____	_____

Use "Previously" *only* when the action was done in the past and no new action was taken this month. Otherwise, all completed actions get counted under "This month."

Carry over actions completed after this month can be reported at the end of the program.

Use a separate sheet to pass on any of the following:
- *personal anecdotes about insights, difficult challenges and their resolution if applicable*
- *resources or ideas you develop, as well as interesting ways of holding meetings and creative ways of communicating the basic information*
- *feedback on the workbook.*

By providing this feedback, you are helping to inspire and motivate others and improve the EcoTeam Program. Thanks for taking the time to make the program work.

Month 4: Improving Transportation Efficiency

Month 4: Improving Transportation Efficiency

Transportation & You

Why transportation is important

Of the two big energy users over which most people in the US have direct control – a house and a car – the car usually has the bigger environmental impact. Private passenger vehicles – cars and light trucks – account for 20% of all energy use in the US, more than all household uses combined.

Not only do cars contribute about 20% of the CO_2 produced in the US, they also emit 34% of the nitrogen oxide that causes acid rain and 27% of the hydrocarbons that cause low-altitude ozone smog. Car air conditioners – which leak and need servicing much more often than home refrigerators – are a major source of CFC emissions, which contribute to global warming and ozone depletion. In addition, cars are a major source of hazardous waste from such things as old engine oil and old batteries.

Highway construction and the sprawling development associated with it gobble up millions of acres a year of farmland, wetlands, and other wilderness, thus contributing to more species extinction.

Thus anything we can do to increase our transportation efficiency – to get the same or better results while using less energy and hazardous materials – will directly benefit the global goals of preserving the atmosphere, reducing waste and preserving biological diversity.

In addition to these environmental impacts, we spend billions of person-hours each year in slow-motion commuting, we lose 50,000 lives to traffic accidents each year, and we subsidize highway transport – through general taxes, health care costs, etc. – by an estimated $2000 per person per year.

Simply put, our society's overdependence on the car is causing us many problems – problems that get worse each year.

The US devotes 43% of its oil use to cars and light trucks, and imports half of its oil.

Improving our transportation efficiency will reduce our dependence on oil imports as well as help the environment.

With this month's actions you could save more than $150 each year for *every* person in you household!

Fortunately, just as with garbage, water, and home energy, there are positive alternatives for transportation that can improve our quality of life while we lower our impact on the environment.

These steps, described in this month's "Action Opportunities," range from personal awareness (such as combining a group of errands into one trip), to proper care for your vehicle so that it can operate at peak performance, to reorganizing your life so that you can live closer to where you work.

Guidelines

- ◆ Reduce your need to drive
- ◆ Get more person-miles out of each gallon of fuel by car pooling and using public transportation
- ◆ Buy the most fuel efficient vehicle that serves your needs and keep it in top condition.

Your goals

- ◆ Get your systems in place to bring environmental balance into your transportation use
- ◆ A reduction of at least 10% of fuel use by the end of the month
- ◆ A reduction of at least 40% of fuel use by the end of the decade.

Earth Day's "Agenda for the Green Decade" has two transportation related goals: a 40% reduction in energy use and a 50% reduction in urban automobile air pollution by the year 2000. Because the actions that individuals can take to reduce automobile air pollution (i.e. burn less fuel) are generally the same as those for reducing energy use, we will focus on the 40% energy use reduction goal.

In absolute terms, current per person energy use for cars is equivalent to about 375 gallons/year. Your goal is to get your household's per person energy for personal transportation down below 225 gallons/year. At a $1.00 a gallon, this can save you $150 per person per year. At higher gas prices, the savings are even greater.

You will be able to estimate how much fuel you use with the help of this month's worksheet, "Assessing Your Fuel Use," on page 79. If your use is quite different from the U.S. average, you may want to adjust your goals. You can either use the 40% reduction goal or you can use the absolute goal of 225 gallons per person per year.

A survey of US business leaders found that half of them felt traffic conditions adversely affected their employees' morale, productivity, punctuality, and emotions.

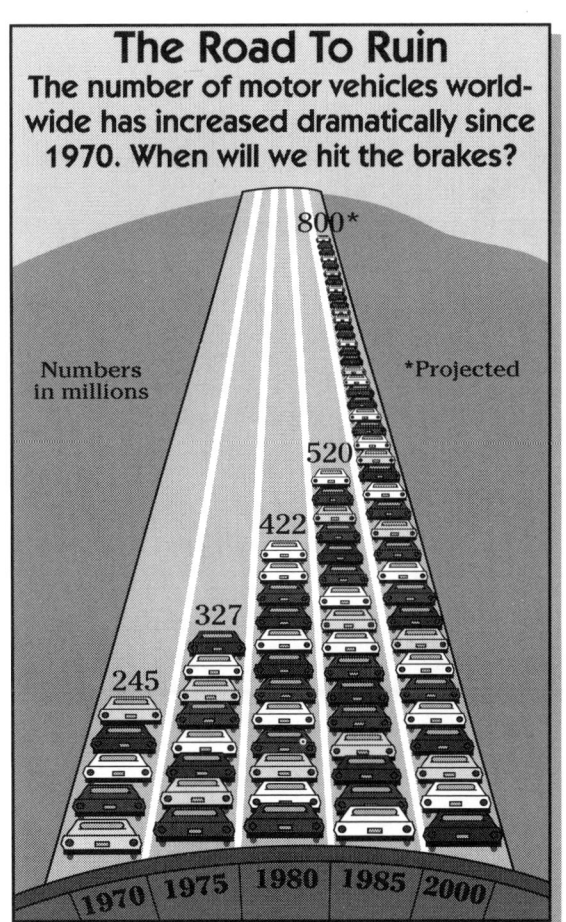

The Road To Ruin
The number of motor vehicles worldwide has increased dramatically since 1970. When will we hit the brakes?

800*

Numbers in millions

*Projected

520

422

327

245

1970 1975 1980 1985 2000

Keeping your water use and energy use records up-to-date gives you clear feedback on your previous months' actions.

This Month's Action Plan

1st week
check-in date
and time

_____

Done ☐

2nd week
check-in date
and time

_____

Done ☐

3rd week
check-in date
and time

_____

Done ☐

1st week

Use the worksheet "Assessing Your Fuel Use" on page 79 to establish how much transportation fuel your household is currently using. At the end of the week check-in, tell the coach how much fuel per person per year your household uses.

2nd week

Use the "Action Opportunities" checklist to look for ways you could save fuel, and pick the opportunities you want to pursue. At the end of the week check-in, tell the coach which actions you've checked as "done before/am doing" and which you "will do."

3rd and 4th weeks

Do it! Complete the action steps that you have selected for this month. At the end of the 3rd week check-in, tell the coach what you are working on.

During the 4th week read over the next chapter, "Month 5: Eco-wise Consumption," in preparation for the next EcoTeam monthly meeting. Transfer any uncompleted actions to the "Carry-Over Actions" chart on page 100.

Remember to keep updating your water use records on Worksheet 2, page 42, and updating your energy use records on Worksheet 3, page 66.

At the next meeting tell this month's coach which specific "Action steps for this month" you have completed.

For guidelines on succeeding with your action plan, see page 21 in Month 1.

Notes

Two railroad tracks can carry as many people as 16 lanes of highway.

Action Opportunities

Reduce your need for travel

The *freedom* to be mobile is wonderful; the necessity to spend hours each day driving isn't. Much of our driving is strictly pragmatic – 75% is devoted to commuting, and running errands. Being more efficient in the way we handle this routine transportation can save time, money and hassle while saving the atmosphere (and leaving the roads freer for more enjoyable driving). Here are some things you can do:

◆ *Combine trips.*

Impulse driving for single errands is an easy way to spend more time in the car than you need to. Multiply this by all the members of your household and before you know it the car is (or cars are) always on the road. The remedy is simple. Before you get in the car always ask everyone else in your household if they are planning any other trips and ask yourself if there is anything else you could do on this trip. Combine all you can.

Action step for this month: Agree in your household to 1) ask the others about their car plans before you go and 2) try to accomplish more than one thing with each trip.

% I am doing ___
% more I will do ___
by (date) _____
Not applicable ☐

Action step done ☐
Date _____ ◆

◆ *Develop alternatives.*

We live in such an auto-centered world that we easily forget there are other ways to get around. Two great fuel savers are walking and biking. Even when these take more time (and in many urban situations they don't), this time provides exercise as well as transport. If you don't have a bicycle, you can borrow or rent one to experiment with this month.

Action step for this month: Find at least one situation where you could walk or bike instead of using your car and try it out.

% I am doing ___
% more I will do ___
by (date) _____
Not applicable ☐

Action step done ☐
Date _____ ◆

Notes

Notes

◆ *Work at home.*

Commuting accounts for about 35% of all car travel. One way that more and more people are reducing their commute is by doing some or all of their work at home. This trend is likely to grow during the decade, and you could be part of it. Even if you worked at home just one day a week, the reduction in your fuel use would be significant.

> **Action step for this month:** If you have a job that could be done at least partly at home, explore the possibilities with your household and your employer.

% I am doing ___
% more I will do ___
by (date) _____
Not applicable ☐

Action step done ☐
Date _____ ◆

◆ *Move closer to work.*

The other way to reduce your commute is to move closer to your work. Remember that you have the whole decade to reach your goal of a 40% reduction in car fuel use, and during the decade chances are good you will move at least once. Plan now that the next time you move (or change jobs) an important consideration will be being close enough to your work so that you could walk, bike or use public transportation.

> **Action step for this month:** Discuss within your household the possibility of living close enough to your work so that you could get to work without needing to use a car.

Done before ☐
I will do ☐
by (date) _____
Not applicable ☐

Action step done ☐
Date _____ ◆

Get more out of each gallon

While the above actions can substantially reduce the amount of time you will need to spend driving, there will still probably be lots of times when you will want the help of a motor vehicle to get around. Here are some ways to make your motor transport more efficient:

◆ *Inflate tires.*

About half the cars in the US have underinflated tires. These soft tires take up to 5% more energy to roll along the road (as well as wearing out faster).

> **Action step for this month:** Get your tires properly inflated.

Done before ☐
I will do ☐
by (date) _____
Not applicable ☐

Action step done ☐
Date _____ ◆

In the Netherlands 30% of work trips, by business people of all kinds, are made by bicycle.

◆ Get a tune-up.

Cars need regular maintenance. If they don't get it, they can become up to 9% less fuel efficient.

Action step for this month: Make an appointment to have a mechanic tune-up your car (or do it yourself).

Done before	☐
I will do	☐
by (date) _____	
Not applicable	☐
Action step done	☐
Date _____ ◆	

◆ Buy a more efficient car.

Some time during the coming decade you will probably buy another car. Since the average fuel efficiency for cars in operation today is only around 21 miles per gallon (mpg), chances are good you could make a big improvement with your next car. How much of an improvement? A 40% improvement over 21 mpg takes you up to 30 mpg – consider that your new minimum. Current models get up to about 50 mpg, and many European and Japanese car companies have prototypes that get 100 mpg and more. You can keep up to date on the latest in car fuel efficiency through publications like *Consumer Reports* (available at most libraries).

Done before	☐
I will do	☐
by (date) _____	
Not applicable	☐

Action step for this month: Look at the *Consumer Reports* annual car survey to find out about currently available fuel-efficient cars. Plan to use this kind of report next time you buy a car.

Action step done	☐
Date _____ ◆	

◆ Use public transportation.

Buses, trains, and other forms of public transport are typically about twice as fuel efficient as car travel. When you add in other costs like parking, insurance, and maintenance, there can be a lot of good reasons for using public transport more often.

% I am doing	___
% more I will do	___
Not applicable	☐

Action step for this month: Find at least one situation where you could use public transportation instead of your car and try it out.

Action step done	☐
Date _____ ◆	

◆ Car pool.

The real measure of transportation efficiency isn't miles per gallon, it's passenger-miles per gallon. Putting more people in the same car is a great way

% I am doing	___
% more I will do	___
Not applicable	☐

Notes

Commuting cars carry an average of less than 1.3 persons per car. All those empty seats fill up the highways.

Notes

to save fuel overall. Many cities and regions have special agencies to help arrange car pooling, and some even provide free car pool vans. Some companies provide car pool assistance as well. You may want to initiate carpooling among your colleagues where you work. Contact the appropriate agency or department to find out more. And car pooling isn't only for work. School activities, evening meetings and recreational outings with friends are just a few examples where a bit more coordination can save a lot more fuel.

Action step for this month: Find at least one situation where you could car pool instead of traveling by yourself and try it out.

Action step done ☐

Date _____◆

As an example, suppose you estimate that starting this month you can combine enough trips to save 7%, you'll inflate your tires for another 5% and you will work at home one day a week for 6%. That's 18% in just this month. For the longer term, you plan to get a more fuel-efficient car, saving 30% plus move closer to work, saving 25%. You now have an overall savings of over 60%!

In the following savings estimator, the numbers for fuel savings give you a rough estimate of the typical impact each action could have if you fully used it. The actual impact of most of these actions will depend strongly on your particular situation and how thoroughly you use each energy-saving strategy. For example, the amount of fuel you save by walking or biking will depend on what percent of your normal driving you displace in this way. Because of this large uncertainty, we suggest you make your own estimates for the likely impact your plans could have in your particular situation. Put these estimates in the "Done Before" and "Will Do" columns, whichever is appropriate. Add up each column to get a rough estimate for your overall savings.

Estimator 7. Savings from transportation actions.

Action for Transportation	Typical % Fuel Savings Up To:	Estimated Savings Done Before	Estimated Savings Will Do	Completion Date
Combine trips	30	_____	_____	_____
Walk or bike	50	_____	_____	_____
Work at home	30	_____	_____	_____
Move closer to work	30	_____	_____	_____
Inflate tires	5	_____	_____	_____
Get a tune-up	9	_____	_____	_____
Buy a more fuel-efficient car	50	_____	_____	_____
Use public transport	20	_____	_____	_____
Car pool	25	_____	_____	_____
Estimated Savings (% of Total)[a]:		_____	_____	

[a] See footnote a, Estimator 1, page 39.

Average passenger-miles per gallon: 27 for air travel, 31 for an urban bus, 37 for a subway, and 110 for an intercity bus.

Worksheet 4: Assessing Your Fuel Use

The purpose of this worksheet is to help you determine how much transportation fuel your household is using. The ideal is to get a full year's history, but less can be all right. Here's how you can do it:

Get your gallons

The "I've got records" method – If you keep detailed records of how much fuel you buy, great. Just add up your total gallons for as many months as you have records. Then go to "Get your yearly" in the next column.

The money method – If you always pay for your fuel with a credit card or check, go back over your credit card statements or check register and add up what you have spent. Divide that by the typical dollars per gallon you pay and you will wind up with total gallons over the time period. For example, if you have paid $600 over the last 6 months and gas costs you $1.20 per gallon, 600 ÷ 1.20 = 500 gallons. Go next to "Get your yearly."

The new records method – If, like many people, you don't keep any records of your purchases, you can still estimate your use by keeping careful records for at least two tankfulls (the longer the better). Put a notebook in your car (or in each of your cars) and record 1) how many gallons you get each time you fill up and 2) when. Use these records to estimate how many gallons per month you are buying. Go next to "Get your yearly."

The mileage method – Look for records that will tell you how many miles you have driven in the past months. When you get your vehicle serviced, the service people usually write down your odometer reading on the bill. Look back at old bills to give you mileage milestones in your past. Read your odometer now and subtract to get the difference. Divide the total miles by your estimate of your vehicle's miles per gallon rate. This will give you total gallons over the time period. For example if you drove 10,000 miles in the past 6

months and your car gets 20 miles to the gallon, 10,000 ÷ 20 = 500 gallons.

Get your yearly

Once you have an estimate for total gallons in some time period, divide the total gallons by the number of months in the time period and then multiply by 12 to get gallons per year. For example, 500 gallons ÷ 6 months = 83 1/3 gallons per month; 83 1/3 gallons per month x 12 = 1000 gallons per year.

For other forms of transportation you can estimate fuel use with the following average factors for passenger-miles per gallon (pmpg): air travel – 27; urban bus – 31; intercity bus – 110; electric railway or subway – 37; taxi or limousine – 15. For each one of these, estimate your total miles traveled in the past year as best you can, then divide by the passenger-miles per gallon factor. For example, 13,500 miles of air travel divided by 27 pmpg = 500 gallons.

Add up your fuel usage for the year from all sources, write the result in the space below and transfer your result to "Before and After Results" on page 98.

Total Yearly Household Fuel Use =

_____ gallons per year

Finally, divide your gallons per year by the number of people in your household to get gallons per year per person. Report this number to your coach at the end of the first week check-in.

Keep a notebook in your car and continue to use it regularly for the rest of this program to get an accurate before and after comparison. Before the last meeting, calculate your new fuel use per year. Transfer your result to "Before and After Results" on page 98.

Notes for the Coach

Before the monthly meeting

1) Read over this chapter of the workbook carefully.

2) Prepare for the monthly meeting. Read over the section on "Facilitating an EcoTeam Meeting" on page 8 for general guidelines and suggestions.

In the monthly meeting

1) Open the meeting in a way that provides insight into this month's theme.

2) Check-in on experiences and results from the previous month.

3) Review with the group the "Action Opportunities" for this chapter of the workbook.

4) Explore the action opportunities. One way to do this is through leading the group in a discussion of successful ways people in the group have reduced their need to drive, and on ways to get more out of each gallon when they do drive.

5) Go over the section "This Month's Action Plan" and make sure everyone understands what to do during the month. Make it clear that at the end of the month you will need to know which specific "Action steps for this month" each household has completed.

Remind your team mates to keep recording their new water usage on Worksheet 2 (page 42) and their new energy use on Worksheet 3 (page 64). Alert them that, in a similar fashion, they will need to keep track of their transportation fuel use over the next few months.

6) Ask who feels they will need help and who would be willing to help. Some team members may anticipate difficulty with part of the process, for example doing the calculations for the worksheet or some of the physical actions. Make sure, for each potential area of difficulty, that everyone feels supported with all the help they need. (Some teams have found it helpful to create a "buddy" system for this purpose.)

7) Invite each of your team members to make a clear commitment, for themselves and for the team, to do this month's action plan.

8) Set up logistics for the weekly check-ins using page 74. Each team member should report progress to the coach on a designated day each week. The coach should compile all of the reports and call each member of the EcoTeam to give them the compiled report.

9) Close with a sense of mutual celebration and support.

At the end of the month

Use the "Coach's Report" to send the GAP Coordination Office a summary of which specific "Action steps for this month" (described at the end of each Action Opportunity) have been taken and by how many households.

> "Success is the sum of small efforts, repeated day in and day out." – Robert Collier

Coach's Report

Please mail or fax a copy of this report to your GAP Coordination Office.

EcoTeam Registration Number: _____

Monthly Coach: _____

Address: _____

_____

Phone: _____

Date: _____   Number of Households in the team: _____

This Month's Action Step:	Number of households that completed this action step:	
	Previously	This month
Discussed combining trips with household (p. 75)	_____	_____
Found at least one situation where walking or biking could be substituted for a car trip (p. 75)	_____	_____
Explored possibilities to work at home (p. 76)	_____	_____
Explored moving to a place where you can get to work without using a car (P. 76)	_____	_____
Checked tires for proper inflation (p. 76)	_____	_____
Made an appointment for a car engine tune up (p. 77)	_____	_____
Found out about available fuel-efficient cars (p. 77)	_____	_____
Used public transportation (p. 77)	_____	_____
Used car pooling (p. 78)	_____	_____

Use "Previously" *only* when the action was done in the past and no new action was taken this month. Otherwise, all completed actions get counted under "This month."

Carry over actions completed after this month can be reported at the end of the program.

Use a separate sheet to pass on any of the following:
- *personal anecdotes about insights, difficult challenges and their resolution if applicable*
- *resources or ideas you develop, as well as interesting ways of holding meetings and creative ways of communicating the basic information*
- *feedback on the workbook.*

By providing this feedback, you are helping to inspire and motivate others and improve the EcoTeam Program. Thanks for taking the time to make the program work.

Month 5: Being an Eco-Wise Consumer

Itinerary for the month:

Month 5: Being an Eco-wise Consumer

Consuming & You

Why consumption is important

Most of our environmental impact is indirect – it is not what we do directly but what is done for us and in our name by business and industry.

For example, only a third of the energy use in the US is under the direct control of individuals in their households and cars; few of us contribute directly to deforestation by cutting down trees; and household water use accounts for only 7.5% of overall water use.

But just because the bulk of our impact is indirect doesn't mean we can't do anything about it. On the contrary, we can shape the environmental behavior of business and industry. And the most powerful way to do this is by changing our buying habits, the topic of this chapter. (We'll explore additional ways in the next chapter on "Empowering Others.")

The deeper goal for this month is to learn a new game - the Eco-wise shopping game.

As living, breathing beings all of us need to consume. We are intentionally using the term "Eco-wise Consumer" – in spite of the objection that some have to the word "consumer" – because we want to openly acknowledge that consumption is a natural part of life. We feel that there is such a thing as "appropriate consumption."

At the same time, we recognize that much of the "consumerism" that has developed in the industrialized world is wasteful of the environment and its resources. This month is intended to help you turn these patterns around and discover what "appropriate consumption" means for you.

The deeper goal for this month is to learn a new game. Most of us have learned the shopping game. In it you "win" by finding items of acceptable quality for the lowest possible price. (Its character as a game becomes clear when you think about the way that most of us play it. Have you ever played it so enthusiastically that you spent great amounts of gasoline and time to score a "bargain"?)

Where does your food come from?
How is it produced, processed and transported?

Guidelines

- Be observant of your motivations for buying
- Choose products
  - with the longest usable life
  - with the least packaging
  - with packaging that is recyclable and biodegradable
  - with the least adverse impact from making and shipping them
    * locally produced
    * no impact on endangered species.
  - that can be recycled or disposed of safely when you're done with them.
- Extend the life of the things you do have through careful maintenance
- Eat lower on the food chain (less meat, eggs and dairy products)
- Grow some of your own food.

Your goals

- Get your systems in place to support buying and consuming habits that are gentler to the Earth
- Reduce your indirect environmental impact through what you buy as you have already reduced your direct household environmental impact.

The Eco-wise shopping game is a little different and may at first seem more complicated than the old game. Quality and price are still important, but in the Eco-wise game it is not just the price on the item that counts. The hidden price paid by the environment is equally important.

The ironic part of the game is that thinking about the Earth while you shop and following the above guidelines will often save you money and time as well as saving the Earth. In those cases where the more ecologically friendly choice is more expensive, it probably reflects a distortion in the economy that fails to count full environmental costs.

The more specific goals for this action area are to change your buying (and not-buying!) habits to reduce your indirect environmental impact just as you have been reducing your direct household impact with the help of the other chapters in this workbook.

Thinking about the Earth while you shop will often save you money and time as well as saving the Earth.

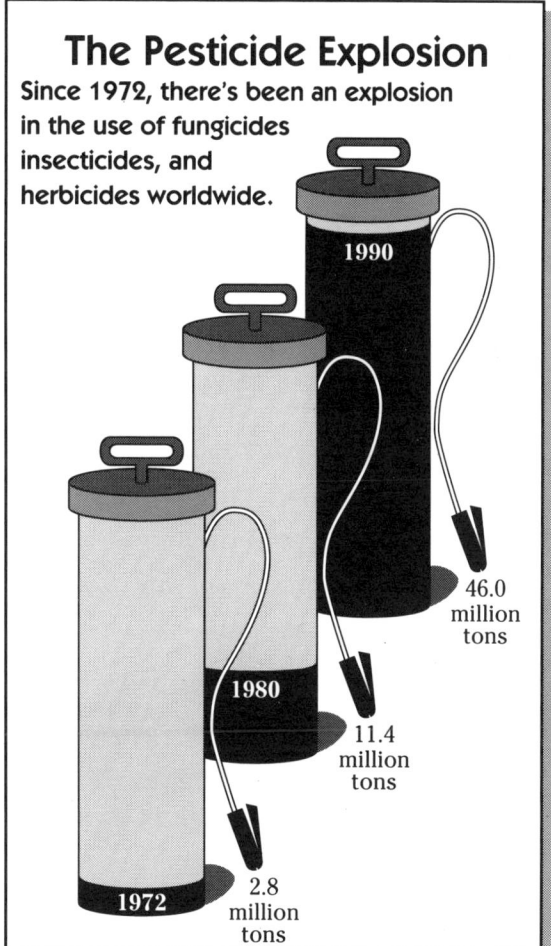

The Pesticide Explosion

Since 1972, there's been an explosion in the use of fungicides insecticides, and herbicides worldwide.

1990 — 46.0 million tons

1980 — 11.4 million tons

1972 — 2.8 million tons

This is the month to determine your "After" results for garbage, water, home energy and fuel use. See Worksheets 1 thru 4.

This Month's Action Plan

Coach's phone number
_____

1st week
check-in date
and time

_____

Done ☐

1st week

Use the "Eco-wise Comparison Shopping" worksheet on page 92 to assess your household's current consuming habits. At the end of the week check-in, tell the coach what you have found.

2nd week
check-in date
and time

_____

Done ☐

2nd week

Use the "Action Opportunities" checklist to look for ways you could change your consuming habits and pick the opportunities you want to pursue. At the end of the week check-in, tell the coach which actions you've checked as "done before/am doing" and which you "will do."

3rd week
check-in date
and time

_____

Done ☐

3rd and 4th weeks

Do it! Complete the action steps that you have selected for this month. At the end of the 3rd week check-in, tell the coach what you are working on.

During the 4th week read over the next chapter, "Month 6: Empowering Others," in preparation for the next EcoTeam monthly meeting. Transfer any uncompleted actions to the "Carry-Over Actions" chart on page 100.

Use Worksheets 1 through 4 to determine your "After" results.

At the next meeting tell this month's coach which specific "Action steps for this month" you have completed.

For guidelines on succeeding with your action plan, see page 21 in Month 1.

At that meeting tell next month's coach your "Before" and "After" results (from page 98) for the End of Program Report. Also be prepared to report any completed "Carry-Over Actions".

Notes

We best honor the Earth and its resources by owning well chosen things of lasting quality.

Action Opportunities

Notes

◆ *Think before you buy.*

From the environment's point of view, two of the biggest ways that we fall into "inappropriate consumption" are 1) buying products as a substitute route to inner fulfillment, and 2) buying low-quality products with short lifetimes.

% I am doing ___
% more I will do ___
Not applicable ☐

What you can do – Before you purchase anything, stop and ask yourself a series of questions:

◆ *What needs and desires do I feel this purchase will serve?* Much of advertising tries to program us into thinking that purchasing a certain product or service will bring more fun into our lives, will make us more loved or more successful, or in some other way will make us "feel good." Ask yourself how much of your desire for this product is based on these advertising-based associations. Think of other ways that you could satisfy these needs, perhaps through something as simple as spending time with a friend.

◆ *Is this purchase a bargain for the Earth?* How long will it last? What are the alternatives that would last longer and have less environmental impact in the long run?

Action steps for this month: With other members of your household, become aware of your motivations for buying things. Discuss what you observe. Also discuss with your household any tendencies your household has to "buy cheap" instead of "buy long-term." Discuss how you might shift to more long-term buying and give each other permission to do so.

Action step done ☐
Date _____ ◆

◆ *Buy in bulk, buy direct, buy local.*

Everything we buy goes through a four-step life. It is first produced, then distributed to us, used by us, and finally disposed. The second step in this chain is a rich source of opportunities for lowering your environmental impact. "Distribution" often involves the long distance transportation of elabo-

% I am doing ___
% more I will do ___
by (date) _____
Not applicable ☐

Bulk buying allows you to shop less often, freeing time for other uses.

rately packaged products, which then sit for weeks in over-lit stores waiting for someone to buy them. You can improve on this by:

- decreasing the volume of packaging by buying in large, family size or bulk quantities
- decreasing the inefficiency of the retail system by buying directly from the producer
- shortening the distance traveled by buying local products.

By doing these things, you will reduce CO_2 emissions from energy use and reduce solid waste from packaging. You will also often save money, time and fuel spent shopping.

What you can do – Look around your house for places you could store bulk supplies, from food to toilet paper. Chances are good that with better organization, a little ingenuity, and maybe a little construction, you could store enough to significantly lower your budget, your environmental impact, and the amount of time you spend shopping. Then find sources of bulk and local products and buy from them.

Action step for this month: Shift at least $50 worth of your monthly purchases to lower-environmental-impact bulk, local or direct items.

Action step done ☐

Date _____ ◆

◆ Keep it maintained

Of the four steps a product goes through, the one with the least environmental impact is usually your use of the product. One of the best ways to increase your quality of life while reducing your environmental impact is to keep using every item you purchase as long as possible. You will reduce the energy used to make and distribute replacement products and you will reduce the volume of discarded products going to the landfill.

% I am doing ___

% more I will do ___

by (date) _____

Not applicable ☐

What you can do – While some maintenance is best done by professionals, there is much that can be done faster as well as cheaper at home. Do you have all the tools and skills you need for simple repair and maintenance – from screwdrivers to sewing machines? If you don't, start adding to your supply of tools, your abilities and your knowledge of friends who

Switching to a diet with less meat, eggs and dairy products is often the one most environmentally positive action you can take.

have particular skills for repair and maintenance. Remember as you do this that there is no need to own every tool. Many tools can be borrowed or rented.

Action steps for this month: Get your household together to inventory your tools, your ability and your knowledge of friends who have particular skills. Agree on guidelines for proper care of your things.

Action step done ☐
Date _____ ◆

◆ *Eat lower on the food chain*

% I am doing ___
% more I will do ___
by (date) _____
Not applicable ☐

This may come as a shock, but frequently the most significant change the average American can make for the sake of the planet is to broaden his or her diet and become less dependent on meat, eggs and dairy products that have come from factory farms and feedlots or from cleared rainforest land. (Please note: We are *not* talking about the nutritional or ethical pros and cons of eating meat, but only about the environmental impact of factory and rainforest farming.)

The reason this is so important is that livestock produced by factory and rainforest farming are very inefficient at converting grains and other resources *that could be used more efficiently for other purposes* into usable food. At the same time, these farms are major sources of pollution, erosion and habitat destruction. Beef is by far the worst, requiring 16 pounds of grain to produce a pound of meat. Dairy on the other hand has a conversion ratio closer to 4 to 1. Consider how this type of farming impacts the global goals:

- ◆ *Preserve the Climate and Atmosphere* – One third of all the raw materials (including energy) consumed in the US is used in the production and distribution of meat, eggs and dairy products. (This includes all related activities, such as growing grains and hay for feed.) In contrast, growing grains, fruits and vegetables for human consumption uses less than 2% of all raw materials. If you were to switch from a standard American diet to one without meat, eggs or dairy products that alone would make a substantial contribution toward achieving the year 2000 goal of reducing your overall per capita CO_2 emission by 35%.

Notes

The difficulty is not meat as such, but the vast expansion of meat production beyond its natural ecological balance.

Notes

- *Preserve the Diversity of Life* – It takes twenty times as much land to feed one person on the standard American diet as it would to feed someone whose diet included no meat, eggs or dairy products. Land freed up by a switch in diet could be used for other purposes, including wildlife habitat. America has already lost 75% of its original topsoil, and we are still losing it at an incredible rate of 60,000 lbs per person per year. Of this loss, 85% is directly associated with the raising of livestock. Topsoil is the fundamental biological resource on which all land species depend.

  More than three times as much meat is derived from formerly-forested land as from original grassland, and that ratio continues to grow. Each hamburger *not* eaten saves half a tree in the tropical rainforests. Producing just one hamburger in the tropics does as much damage to the forests as producing the paper for 350 grocery bags! Cattle raising is responsible for at least 12% of the clearing of tropical forests, and leaves the ex-forest land in even worse shape than the other major sources of deforestation, slash and burn agriculture and logging. Tropical rainforests are estimated to be the home of fully half of all species on Earth. Their destruction is a major cause of species extinction.

- *Use Water Wisely* – Meat, egg and dairy production (including related feed production) account for about 3/4 of all the water usage in the US. Eating only 7 lbs less beef per year (less than 10% of the American per capita average) would be the same as reducing per capita household water use by 33% (the Earth Day goal). Animal wastes account for more than ten times as much water pollution as that attributable to the human population. The meat industry accounts for three times as much harmful organic pollution as all the rest of the nation's industries.

- *Stabilize Humanity* – The world's cattle alone consume enough food to supply the caloric intake of 8.7 billion people – the level of population the world may stabilize at in few decades.

  What you can do – Use the "Eco-wise Comparison Shopping" worksheet on page 92 to assess the envi-

An organic garden is an oasis for beneficial wildlife as well as a gift of health for you.

ronmental impact of your food buying habits. Get some cookbooks with recipes that are low in meat, eggs and dairy products, and find some local restaurants that serve similar meals. Explore and expand your horizons.

Action step for this month: At least once a week, replace a meat-oriented meal with a fish or vegetarian meal and plan to reduce your long term consumption of factory and rainforest farm products even further.

Action step done ☐
Date _____ ◆

◆ Grow your own food

Home grown food is not only frequently fresher and nutritionally better for you, it is also better for the environment. Because of the greater personal care gardeners give to their work, they can regularly produce 4 to 6 times more food per square foot than a professional farmer, and they usually do it with little or no chemical fertilizer, pesticides, or soil erosion. In addition, home grown food eliminates all of the energy used and pollution generated by commercial food processing and distribution, and often uses much less water. Growing your own food thus helps to preserve the atmosphere by reducing energy use, preserve the diversity of life by reducing the amount of land needed for agriculture, reduce solid waste by eliminating the need for packaging, and reduce water use and pollution.

% I am doing ____
% more I will do ____
by (date) _____
Not applicable ☐

What you can do – Assess your options for growing some of your own food. Even in an apartment, you can grow sprouts in jars. Many urban areas also have community gardens. If growing things appeals to you, there are many ways you can do it. With a little searching you can probably find friends who would be glad to help you get started.

Action step for this month: Take some action (appropriate to the season) toward growing some of your own food.

Action step done ☐
Date _____ ◆

Worksheet 5: Eco-Wise Comparison Shopping

Notes for "Eco-Wise Comparison Shopping"

Purpose of this worksheet: To raise your awareness about the different environmental impacts that your shopping choices have. (No calculations this time!)

How to use this worksheet

1) Take it (or a copy of it) with you next time you go shopping. The examples given here are for food, but it could be adapted for anything, from clothing to electronic gadgets.

2) Begin with an item you usually buy. Mark down its

- size (in oz., lbs., quarts, etc.)
- price
- unit price (in $ per lb, etc. – often marked on the shelf in the same place as the item's price)
- packaging (Is it paper, plastic, or some composite? Could you recycle it?)
- impact notes (Is it produced locally or does it come from far away? How much pollution is caused by the way it is produced? Can it be recycled? Can it be disposed safely? If you don't know, put in a "?" and find out more later.)

3) Look for alternatives that might have a lower environmental impact through

- larger size (less packaging per unit weight)
- a more recyclable packaging (e.g. cardboard instead of a composite)
- locally produced, or food that is in season (less transportation)
- simply not buying anything!

4) Use the next line(s) on the worksheet to mark down the corresponding information for the most environmentally friendly alternative(s). (If your normal item is the most environmentally friendly product available, you might compare this to the *least* environmentally friendly alternative.)

5) Keep going down the worksheet filling in information for 1) your normal purchases and then 2) more environmentally friendly alternatives.

Example

Item	Size	Price	Unit Price	Packaging	Impact Notes
Clothes detergent	4 lb	$2.54	$0.64/lb	cardboard	
Same brand/larger size	25 lb	$11.89	$0.48/lb	cardboard	less packaging/lb & cheaper
Jam/national brand	10 oz	$2.49	$3.98/lb	glass	
Jam/local brand	15 oz	$3.12	$3.33/lb	glass	local & cheaper

How long will this product last?
What will happen to it when you are done with it?

Eco-wise Comparison Shopping

Item	Size	Price	Unit Price	Packaging	Impact Notes

"[We] can not shuffle off our responsibility upon the shoulders of God or nature. ... It is up to us." – Arnold Toynbee

Notes for the Coach

Before the monthly meeting

1) Read this chapter carefully.

2) Prepare for the monthly meeting. Read the section on "Facilitating an EcoTeam Meeting" on page 8 for general guidelines and suggestions.

In the monthly meeting

1) Open the meeting in a way that provides insight into this month's theme.

2) Check-in on experiences and results from the previous month.

3) Review with the group the "Action Opportunities" for this chapter of the workbook.

4) Do a house tour, demonstration, and/or lead a discussion. Here are some possibilities:

Encourage a discussion of what EcoTeam members have observed about their own motivations for purchasing and what has influenced their buying habits.

Facilitate a discussion of ways people have extended the life of their things through careful maintenance and repair. How do team members feel about being able to give reverent care to things they enjoy? What obstacles, particularly inner ones, did they have to overcome to develop their ability to care for things?

Use the creativity of the group to look for unusual ways to expand the storage space in the house where the meeting takes place. One of the biggest obstacles to bulk buying is the limiting belief "but I don't have anywhere to store things." Look for unused or poorly used space under clothes in closets, under beds and other furniture, and elsewhere. Look for places where simple shelves could expand storage capacity.

Bring some vegetarian cookbooks (like the *Moosewood* series or *Laurel's Kitchen*) for people to look through. Encourage those in the group who have experience with low-meat or vegetarian meals to share what they have learned.

5) Go over the section "This Month's Action Plan" and make sure everyone understands what to do during the month. Make it clear that at the end of the month you will need to know which specific "Action steps for this month" each household has completed.

Remind your teammates that during this month they should use Worksheets 1 through 4 a second time to determine their "After" results for garbage, water, home energy and fuel use so that they can report these results at the next meeting. Completed "Carry-Over" actions can also be reported at the next meeting.

6) Ask who feels they will need help and who would be willing to help. Some team members may anticipate difficulty with part of the process, for example using the worksheet. Make sure, for each potential area of difficulty, that everyone feels supported with all the help they need.

7) Invite each of your team members to make a clear commitment, for themselves and for the team, to do this month's action plan.

8) Set up logistics for the weekly check-ins using page 86. Each team member should report progress to the coach on a designated day each week. The coach should compile all of the reports and call each member of the EcoTeam to give them the compiled report.

9) Close with a sense of mutual celebration and support.

At the end of the month

Use the "Coach's Report" to send the GAP Coordination Office a summary of which specific "Action steps for this month" (described at the end of each Action Opportunity) have been taken and by how many households.

"A little and little, collected together, become a great deal; the heap in the barn consists of single grains." – Hesiod

Coach's Report

Please mail or fax a copy of this report to your GAP Coordination Office.

EcoTeam Registration Number: _____

Monthly Coach: _____

Address: _____

_____

Phone: _____

Date: _____ Number of Households in the team: _____

	Number of households that completed this action step:	
This Month's Action Step:	**Previously**	**This month**
Discussed motivation for buying with household (p. 87)	_____	_____
Shifted $50 of monthly purchases to lower impact (p. 88)	_____	_____
Inventoried tools and skills for repairs (p. 89)	_____	_____
Replaced one meat-oriented meal a week (p. 91)	_____	_____
Took some action to begin growing own food (p. 91)	_____	_____

Use a separate sheet to pass on any of the following:

- *personal anecdotes about insights, difficult challenges and their resolution if applicable*
- *resources or ideas you develop, as well as interesting ways of holding meetings and creative ways of communicating the basic information*
- *feedback on the workbook.*

By providing this feedback, you are helping to inspire and motivate others and improve the EcoTeam Program. Thanks for taking the time to make the program work.

End of Program Report

In this chapter:

End of Program Report

We calculate yearly rates here to provide consistency within GAP and with other statistics. These rates are an extrapolation based on your actions during the program. Clearly, you must maintain your new behavior to continue to get these savings.

This worksheet is important for two reasons:

♦ The results in it are the core of the quantitative feedback GAP is gathering to measure progress towards the global environmental goals. These results, even with their approximations, provide important and useful information.

♦ The worksheet will give you a clear summary of the personal impact your actions have had toward bringing your household into environmental balance.

At the start of each of the first four months you are asked to complete a worksheet to assess your environmental impact before your participation in the EcoTeam Program, and transfer your "before" results here to "Before and After Results"

To get full value from the program you need to again use the worksheets from the first four months, but this time to determine your "after" results. If you have not already done that, do so before the end of the fifth month and the sixth meeting. You will be asked at that last meeting to let your coach know your "before" and "after" results so that these can go into the "Coach's End of Program Report."

Once you have all your "before" and "after" results on this worksheet, you can use these numbers to calculate your yearly personal positive environmental impact from the program. Here's how:

In these sidebars are examples for a typical household of 4 people.

Landfill garbage (lbs per household per week, from Worksheet 1 column 2, page 26)

1) Subtract the "after" number from the "before" number to get your net savings.

2) Divide the net savings by the "before" number to get your percent savings.

3) Since the "before" and "after" numbers are in lbs per week, you need to multiply the net savings by 52 (weeks in a year) to get yearly savings in lbs per year.

4) Divide the yearly savings by 30 lbs per cubic foot (typical landfill density) to give the cubic feet of landfill you have saved. (A cinder block occupies 0.6 cubic feet.)

5) Divide the landfill saved by a further factor of 10 (or yearly savings by 300) to give you the average number of trees you have saved by either recycling or not consuming paper products.

Garbage:
  80 before
  - 20 after
  = 60 net.

60 ÷ 80 = 75%

60 x 52 = 3,120

3,120 ÷ 30 = 104

104 ÷ 10 = 10.4

_____ **before the program** (*report this to the coach*)

− _____ **after the program** (*report this to the coach*)

= _____ net savings   (÷ "before" = _____% savings)

x 52 = _____ yearly savings

÷ 30 = _____ cubic feet of landfill saved per year

÷ 10 = _____ trees saved per year

Water use (gallons per household per day, from Worksheet 2, page 42)

1) Subtract the "after" number from the "before" number to get your net savings.

This short but important chapter is the place where you keep track of your overall progress. It is your headquarters.

2) Divide the net savings by the "before" number to get your percent savings.

3) Since the "before" and "after" numbers are in gallons per day, you need to multiply the net savings by 365 to get yearly savings in gallons per year.

<pre>
_____   before the program (report this to the coach)
– _____   after the program (report this to the coach)
= _____   net savings   (÷ "before" = _____% savings)
x 365 = _____   yearly savings
</pre>

Water:

600 before
- 400 after
= 200 net.

200 ÷ 600 = 33%

200 x 365 = 73,000

Home CO_2 output (lbs per household per year, from Worksheet 3, page 64)

1) Subtract the "after" number from the "before" number to get your net savings.

2) Divide the net savings by the "before" number to get your percent savings.

<pre>
_____   before the program (report this to the coach)
– _____   after the program (report this to the coach)
= _____   yearly savings (÷ "before" = _____% savings)
</pre>

Home CO_2:

31,600 before
- 22,120 after
= 9,480 net.

9,480 ÷ 31,600 = 30%

Transport fuel use (gallons per household per year, from Worksheet 4, page 79)

1) Subtract the "after" number from the "before" number to get your net savings.

2) Divide the net savings by the "before" number to get your percent savings.

<pre>
_____   before the program (report this to the coach)
– _____   after the program (report this to the coach)
= _____   yearly savings (÷ "before" = _____% savings)
</pre>

Fuel:

1,500 before
- 900 after
= 600 net.

600 ÷ 1,500 = 40%

Total CO_2 savings (lbs per household per year)

1) Multiply your transport fuel savings by 22 to convert it into CO_2 savings.

2) Add this to your home CO_2 savings to estimate your total CO_2 savings.

Yearly transport fuel savings x 22 = _____

Yearly home CO_2 savings = _____

add these to get total CO_2 savings = _____

Total CO_2:

600 x 22 = 13,200

13,200
+9,480
22,680

Total dollar savings (per household per year)

1) Divide your total CO_2 savings by 22 to convert it back to equivalent fuel gallons, then multiply by your average fuel cost.

2) Multiply your water savings by your water cost (in dollars per gallon).

3) Add these for an estimated total savings.

Yearly CO_2 savings x fuel cost ÷ 22= _____

Yearly water savings x water cost = _____

add these to get the total = _____ (report this to the coach)

Dollars:

22,680 ÷ 22 = 1,031

1,031 x $1.10 = $1,134

73,000 x $.001 = $73

$1,134
+73
$1,207

All of these savings estimates underestimate your full savings because they do not include the indirect effect of negative environmental impacts avoided by your new Eco-wise buying habits, or the dollar savings from these new buying habits.

Carry-Over Actions

You might want to photocopy this page and put it in a prominent place, like the door of your refrigerator.

Use this page to keep track of actions that you were not able to complete during their month. At the end of each month, fill in a brief description of any uncompleted actions along with their page numbers. Set a target date for when you plan to complete each action, and once you have completed a particular action, fill in the completion date.

Compile your completed carry-over actions before the last meeting so they can be reported to the coach and included in the End of Program feedback to GAP.

Target date	Completion date	Page #	Action description

"If we triumph in the little things of our common hours, we are sure to triumph in our lives" – Anonymous

Coach's End of Program Report

Please mail or fax a copy of this report to your GAP Coordination Office.

This report is to be filled out by the Month 6 Coach. Please see the Month 6 Notes for the Coach on page 121.

EcoTeam Registration Number: _____

Monthly Coach: _____

Address: _____

_____

Phone: _____

Date: _____ Number of Households in the team: _____

Household			Garbage Landfill (lbs per week)		Water Total Use (gals per day)		Energy CO_2 Output (lbs per year)		Transport Fuel Use (gals per year)		Dollar Savings (per year)
Member Name		Number in Household	Before	After	Before	After	Before	After	Before	After	After
1.											
2.											
3.											
4.											
5.											
6.											
7.											
8.											
9.											
10.											
11.											
12.											
13.											
14.											
15.											
Totals:											

Month 6: Empowering Others

Month 6: Empowering Others

How this chapter works

This chapter and the month it supports differ from the previous five in important ways. It serves as a bridge between the actions you have been taking within your household and the actions you can take beyond your household. It invites you to use what you have learned and adapt it to empowering others at the household, workplace and community levels.

Activating Other Household EcoTeams: Guidelines for being a catalyst for others to use this program.

Bringing Your Workplace Into Environmental Balance: Guidelines for applying the principles in the Household EcoTeam Program to your workplace. It includes a Workplace Environmental Audit.

Bringing Your Community Into Environmental Balance: Similar guidelines and environmental audit for your community.

Guidelines for Empowering Others: Approaches that can be used at all three levels.

The meeting at the start of the month is the last in the program, so the chapter also supports appropriate closure for this part of your team's journey.

Person by Person

Why empowering others is important

It is probably clear to you by now that some of the things that need to be done are beyond the domain of your household. How can you take what you have learned and help restore the larger environment in which you live? Empowering others to take responsibility for the health of our Earth is the obvious next step.

Change happens person-by-person. There is no other way. One person taking responsibility inspires another, who passes it along to another until we have a community of people committed to change. By now you have overcome the resistances that inhibit action. When you talk to another you are speaking from experience. People will listen!

This section of the workbook suggests possible next steps you can take to help heal our Earth. As you know, we are living

The next step of the process is *you* carrying the torch and enabling another.

in the critical decade which will determine the habitability of our Earth for our children's and grandchildren's generations. Every action taken or not taken today will determine the quality of life available to them. Every person willing to stand up now and be counted, while we still have time to influence things, has considerable leverage in determining the future for our planet. This is a very special opportunity that comes along rarely in history.

The GAP EcoTeam Program has helped you take responsibility. The next step of the process is *you* carrying the torch and enabling another. The success of GAP is based on you speaking to another – it's totally grass-roots initiated. If you are willing to take the next step out beyond your own house, the Global Action Plan for the Earth will expand and help restore our environment; if you're not, it will languish. It's that simple. You make the difference! You can actively continue to support the restoration of our environment by the following three actions:

1) *Create more Household EcoTeams.* This is the building block for environmental change: person-by-person, household-by-household. There are endless opportunities to speak to people you know or to different groups and encourage them to form Household EcoTeams.

2) *Bring your workplace into environmental balance.* This is the next level, the creating of a Workplace EcoTeam. Our workplaces account for the majority of negative impact on the environment. Environmentally responsible practices must be instituted in the workplace if we are to achieve long-term viability for our planet.

3) *Bring your community into environmental balance.* As you went through this workbook in all likelihood you noticed environmental issues beyond the domain of your household and workplace that require community action. Initiating the needed community environmental changes or assisting with what is already under way could be a natural outgrowth of your present EcoTeam. Since it is already formed, bonded and feeling empowered, it can be a major catalyst in the community change process.

The sections that follow provide possible blueprints for empowering others at the household, workplace, and community levels.

Your goal

To support each member of the EcoTeam in taking his or her next step in caring for the Earth, either individually or as part of the existing team's next action.

Environmentally responsible practices must be instituted in the workplace if we are to achieve long-term viability for our planet.

Activating Other Household EcoTeams

The building block to restore our environment is you and me living a lifestyle in balance with the needs of the Earth. As we change, the world begins to change. There are countless opportunities for each of us to help one another bring about these essential environmental changes. The following guidelines will assist you.

1) Reaching out to another is a natural process of wanting to share something that has been meaningful to you. It's very possible you have already started doing this spontaneously. As you begin talking to others note that there are many reasons an individual might be motivated to participate – to express concern about the environment, to save money, to have an experience of community, to make a difference, to be part of a worldwide grass-roots movement and so on. We are all different. As you speak to someone, try to get a sense of what's important to them and build on that.

2) In addition to spontaneous conversations, there are more structured opportunities you can create to talk about the Household EcoTeam Program. Invite people you know to your house for dinner, speak to a group that meets regularly, speak on a local radio show, put up notices around town and give a talk. There are endless ways to connect with people.

3) In communicating about the program, use the first part of this workbook "About the Household EcoTeam Program" to explain the purpose and structure. Then tell your own story. This is what will be most compelling for others. Tell them about:

Consider the impact of your helping form ten or fifty or a hundred EcoTeams – the multiplication effect is quite remarkable.

- What you have accomplished
- What you have learned
- The changes you have made
- The money you've saved
- The personal insights you have gleaned
- The experience of community you have had.

You will be an inspiration to others. So many people today are looking for help in translating their environmental awareness into action. You and the Household EcoTeam Program are providing that bridge.

4) When someone decides to form a Household EcoTeam put them in touch with your GAP Coordinator so that they can get their Workbook and get going.

5) Take time to reflect on the environmental impact of your helping form just one other EcoTeam. That person will go out and connect with 8 to 12 people. Consider the impact of your helping form ten or fifty or a hundred EcoTeams – the multiplication effect is quite remarkable. Consider the positive impact that will begin to occur in your community. As one person, you can make quite an extraordinary difference if you are so inspired.

6) The process of activating other Household EcoTeams can be done by you alone, with parts of your present EcoTeam, or as a project of the whole EcoTeam. If you proceed as an EcoTeam, arrange monthly meetings to support your process. Also, remember to use the feedback component of GAP and do your weekly check-ins on progress.

7) Report in monthly, via phone or mail, to your GAP Coordinator with the number of Household EcoTeams you have helped start and to hear about the progress of others doing the same.

The benefits you can provide your workplace are substantive and valuable.

Bringing Your Workplace Into Environmental Balance

After putting your own house in order you will inevitably notice what needs to be done in your workplace (assuming it's in a different location). Bringing your workplace into environmental balance requires you to do many of the same things you did at the household level. Some of these changes will be relatively easy to initiate as they are primarily related to raising consciousness and often will save money. Others will be more complex as their resolution will require a long term shift in economic priorities. The way this long term reprioritization will occur however, is by raising the environmental consciousness workplace by workplace. Your actions therefore have great leverage potential. Once again, you make a difference!

Although it might be initially challenging to overcome the inertia and established routines of those you work with, the benefits you are providing – cost savings, health protection, work spirit, environmental responsibility, etc. – are substantive and will be valued if presented properly. The model suggested for workplace mobilization is the same social empowerment strategy GAP has utilized at the household and global level:

♦ *Education* as to what the problem is, and in the skills necessary to bring about the needed change

♦ A concrete vision of what is to be accomplished translated into *measurable action goals*

♦ Regular *feedback* showing how the action is achieving the goals.

The following is an example of how the social empowerment strategy can be used.

♦ An individual attempted to get her fellow workers to switch from drinking coffee out of paper cups to drinking out of mugs. She tried the usual mobilization strategy imploring people to change and was unsuccessful. She then used the social empowerment strategy.

♦ On the community bulletin board noticeable to everyone when they came in to work, she posted how many trees they consumed in the last month by drinking their coffee out of paper cups. (Education about the problem)

♦ The next week she posted on the bulletin board the goal that people bring a mug in to work and indicate participation by signing their name on the affixed list. (Goal that is quantifiable and measurable)

♦ Each day more and more people signed the sheet and by the end of the first week, 25% of her fellow workers had made commitments. (Feedback showing how each person was making a difference and the collective result being achieved)

♦ By the end of the third week all the people working there had brought a mug in to work and the change was instituted.

Utilizing the social empowerment strategy the following are key steps in mobilizing environmental change in your workplace:

1) The first step is to form a Workplace EcoTeam with like-minded colleagues. This might be done under the umbrella of an environmental task force. Encourage

The idea is to make sure the changes are done gradually so as not to overwhelm people and the systems.

The more fun the whole process is for you and your EcoTeam the greater the chances it will be fun for others.

It's important that you appeal to others in a way that empowers them. It's easy to fall into the trap of appealing to guilt. We're all in this new learning together!

members of your EcoTeam to set up Household EcoTeams for their own sake, and so they can get a more personal experience of the process.

2) Then, do a workplace environmental audit to assess what is needed and what is presently being done to address these issues. A workplace audit checklist is provided at the end of this section to assist your EcoTeam in this process.

3) After you have completed the audit and determined what needs to be changed to bring your workplace into environmental balance, create a plan of action. (If you would like assistance for this and the workplace change process, contact the GAP National Coordination Office for information about the Corporate Environmental Leadership Program.) In developing this plan, consider:

- *A Workplace Agenda for the Green Decade* A set of goals that needs to be achieved. Where possible link them into the Earth Day global "Agenda for the Green Decade."

- *A timeframe for completion* You might want to set up a goal a month and adapt the format designed for the Household EcoTeams. The idea is to make sure the changes are done gradually so as not to overwhelm people and the systems. As the rest of your workplace colleagues catch on, the process will start to generate momentum.

- *A social empowerment strategy* When you are encouraging a change in behavior of many of your colleagues, remember to educate, set a goal, and provide feedback. Be creative in designing your strategy and have fun. In fact, the more fun the whole process is for you and your EcoTeam the greater the chances it will be fun for others. It's important that you appeal to others in a way that empowers them. It's easy to fall into the trap of appealing to guilt. We're all in this new learning together!

- *Keep everyone informed of overall progress* Where you need to speak to just several key decision-makers, inform the rest of your workplace community of results achieved. This gives your colleagues feedback and encourages them to be active in the areas where they have more direct control to influence change.

4) Please provide your Coordination Office with a monthly status report of your progress, via phone or mail, so we can communicate it to the other Workplace EcoTeams. As successes at the various stages begin to accrue they will be of great value in motivating others.

Note – With a little adaptation this section could be utilized by young people to help bring their school (since that is their workplace) into environmental balance. As interest grows in this area, we will develop a school component of our workplace feedback system.

Where does the energy used in your workplace come from?

Worksheet 7: Workplace Environmental Audit

Introduction:

Workplaces are the next level of organization that most of us influence beyond our households. Begin by assessing the current state of your workplace, similarly to the way you began in your household.

- What are the key issues that need to be addressed in your workplace?
- What are your workplace's current environmental impacts in those areas?
- What goals should your workplace be aiming for in those areas?
- What, if anything, is already being done toward achieving those goals?
- What more needs to be done?

The Earth Day global goals can be a great help toward answering both what the key issues are and what your workplace goals should be. Using those goals and what we have already done in the household, we expect that for most workplaces the key issue areas will include:

- waste
- water use
- energy use
- transportation
- eco-wise production
- eco-wise purchasing.

For each one of these areas we have suggested a few questions that can provide a starting point for doing an environmental audit of your workplace. You will want to add additional questions based on major issues for your workplace that are not addressed by this list and on your awareness of additional action opportunities.

Waste

Waste Production. How much solid waste does your workplace send to the landfill?

Total Production _____

Paper.
> Does your workplace minimize the use of paper, reuse it by printing on both sides, and recycle it?

Recycling.
> Does your workplace have an adequate recycling program?
>
> How much of the total waste stream gets recycled?

Could your workplace replace some of its common toxics with non-toxic alternatives, as you have done in your household?

Notes

Hazardous Materials.

Does your workplace have adequate programs for reducing the use of hazardous materials, recycling them when they are used, and disposing of them properly when recycling is not possible?

Water

Water Use. How much water does your workplace use? How is this use distributed among office use, production, etc.?

Total Use _____; Segments (%) _____

For Employees.

Do your workplace bathrooms, kitchens, etc. have water efficient toilets, faucets, etc. similar to those discussed for the household?

Production and Washing.

If your workplace uses water in its production process or for washing goods or equipment, is this being done efficiently?

Energy

Energy Use. How much energy does your workplace use? How is this use distributed among office use, transportation, production, or any specialized uses?

Total Use _____; Segments (%) _____

Heating & Cooling.

Are your buildings well insulated?

Do they take full advantage of solar heating?

Hot Water.

Is your workplace making full use of sources like waste heat or solar heating for its hot water needs?

Is all piping well insulated?

Equipment.

Does your workplace have energy-efficient equipment?

Is someone in your workplace keeping up on efficiency improvements for your major energy-using equipment?

Lighting.

Does your workplace have energy-efficient lighting?

Is someone in your workplace keeping up on efficiency improvements for lighting?

Lifecycle design is the wave of the future. It is none too soon to start now.

Transportation

Employee Commuting.

Does your workplace make it easy for employees to get to work by some means other than a car?

Does it support working at home?

Business Travel, Shipping & Receiving.

Does your workplace coordinate trips and errands to reduce travel?

Is it flexible in scheduling so that rush-hour and congestion can be avoided in deliveries and errands?

Eco-wise Production

Lifecycle Design.

Does your workplace design its products or services to minimize their environmental impact throughout the full lifecycle from raw materials to final disposal?

Are the products designed for long life and easy servicing?

Are they designed to be easily recycled?

Packaging.

Does your workplace design the packaging for its products to minimize its environmental impact?

Is CFC emitting foam avoided?

Is the packaging designed for easy recycling?

Servicing.

Does your workplace provide servicing that extends the life of its products?

Does it assist others in performing this servicing?

Eco-wise Purchasing

Purchasing Awareness.

Do the purchasing agents at your workplace include environmental considerations in the choice of products and supplies?

Do they choose products with the longest usable life?

With the least packaging?

With packaging that is recyclable and/or biodegradable?

With the least known adverse impact from making and shipping them?

That can be recycled or disposed safely when you are done with them?

Bringing Your Community Into Environmental Balance

Within two days, the people of Adelaide had obtained cooperation from 40% of the grocery stores and supermarkets. By the end of the week they had a 100% response.

Bringing about changes at the community level, where you interact with other people, groups, and often conflicting agendas, requires much in the way of people skills and an effective mobilization strategy. GAP recommends using the same social empowerment strategy that we've used at the household, workplace, and global level. For your review, its three elements are:

♦ *Education* as to what the problem is and in the skills necessary to bring about the needed change

♦ A concrete vision of what is to be accomplished translated into *measurable action goals*

♦ Regular *feedback* showing results being achieved in relationship to the goals.

A successful application of this social empowerment strategy took place in Adelaide, Australia.

♦ A concerned individual contacted a local radio station and suggested the station conduct an environmental campaign on the ozone hole, since this is causing serious health hazards to Australians right now.

♦ In the first week the radio station communicated to listeners that CFCs released into the atmosphere caused a hole in the ozone. They noted that Styrofoam packaging and cups were one of the products that contained CFCs. (Education about the problem – the "what")

♦ The second week they proposed to their listeners *a very specific goal that was measurable and quantifiable.* Go to your local grocery store and supermarket and ask them to remove all Styrofoam packaging and cups from their shelves and refrain from ordering more in the future. (Education for effective action – the "how")

♦ Then call the radio station and it will broadcast the results of this action each day. (Feedback)

♦ Within two days, the people of Adelaide had obtained cooperation from 40% of the grocery stores and supermarkets. By the end of the week they had a 100% response. All Styrofoam packaging and cups were removed from all grocery stores and supermarkets in Adelaide.

Utilizing this social empowerment strategy, the following are key steps to take in mobilizing environmental change in your community:

1) A Household EcoTeam or group of EcoTeams meet and conduct a community environmental audit to determine the status of the community. This will determine what is needed and what is presently being done about it. To assist this assessment process a community audit checklist is provided at the end of this section.

2) Based on this assessment, the Eco-Team invites the community's environmental leadership to create a local version of the "Agenda for the Green Decade" – community environmental goals to be achieved over the decade of the 1990s. The majority of these goals will likely align with the global goals of Earth Day's agenda. There may be a number, however, which will be appropriate only for your community. Developing these goals will create a process of alignment among the different players – if you accomplish this, half the work will be done! The other half

Developing community environmental goals will create a process of alignment among the different players.

will be to mobilize the community to achieve these goals – equally no small task! But by now your Community Eco-Team will have created substantial momentum and hopefully considerable enthusiasm.

3) The next part of the mobilization strategy is two-fold:

- ◆ Encourage those groups who are working on restoring some part of the environment to begin measuring their actions in relationship to the community's "Agenda for the Green Decade."

- ◆ Where nothing is being done, encourage one or more household EcoTeams to take responsibility for that environmental issue. Ask your GAP Coordinator for a list of other EcoTeams in your area.

4) Once the concerned individuals are involved, the next step is to develop a feedback system that gives regular reports on progress. Earth Day each year is a logical time to give the major progress report of what was achieved in the previous year and to present the goals for the upcoming year. There will, however, need to be more frequent feedback around specific campaigns underway during the year.

5) Using the example of Adelaide, Australia, develop a working relationship with the news media in the various campaigns. Start with campaigns that are simple so you can build on success.

6) When underwriting for particular campaigns is needed, a possible source may be locally environmentally-conscious businesses. Encourage a three-way partnership between the business community, the media outlet(s) providing the feedback, and yourself as the Community EcoTeam.

7) Once the components of the social empowerment strategy are understood (education, goals, feedback), designing the particular campaigns and funding strategies is a function of creativity, good people skills and hard work.

8) Please provide your Coordination Office with a monthly status report of your progress, via phone or mail, so we can communicate it to the other Community EcoTeams around the world. Even if it's modest, it inspires others to know where you are in your process and how you are addressing the challenges you face. Another Community EcoTeam may be in a similar place and your communication may be just what they need to take the next step. The reverse is also true – their communication may be just what your Eco-Team needs to take the next step. The feedback process is designed to be mutually reinforcing and help the whole change process build upon itself. We will also collect your feedback and use it to help future Community EcoTeams.

Encourage those groups who are working on restoring some part of the environment to begin measuring their actions in relationship to the community's "Agenda for the Green Decade."

Notes

Worksheet 8: Community Environmental Audit

Introduction

While communities are more complex than households or workplaces, the basic steps required to bring your community into environmental balance have much in common with the steps you have taken for your household. You need to begin by assessing the current state of your community:

♦ What are the key issues that need to be addressed?

♦ What are the community's current environmental impacts in those areas?

♦ What goals should the community be aiming for in those areas?

♦ Who is already working toward those goals?

♦ What more needs to be done?

The Earth Day global goals can be a great help toward answering both what the key issues are and what your community goals should be. Using those goals and what we have already done in the household, we expect that for most communities the key issue areas will include:

♦ waste

♦ water use

♦ energy use

♦ air quality

♦ transportation

♦ species and habitat preservation.

For each one of these areas we have suggested a few questions that can provide a starting point for doing an environmental audit of your community. You will want to add additional questions based on major issues for your community that are not addressed by this list and on your awareness of additional action opportunities.

To answer many of these questions you will need to reach out into your community, getting information from local government and community groups. Since these groups and local government will need to be part of any successful action plan, begin to build relationships as you do this assessment. Better yet, bring these others in as partners in the process of creating the assessment.

Waste

Waste Production. How much solid waste does your overall community send to the landfill? What is your community's per person garbage production? How does that compare with the Earth Day goal of less than 250 lbs per person per year by 2000?

Total Use _____ ; Per Person Use _____

Is your community pursuing any of the innovative biological approaches to water purification?

Recycling.

> Does your community have an adequate recycling program?

> How much of the total waste stream gets recycled?

Hazardous Materials.

> Does your community have adequate programs for reducing the use of hazardous materials, recycling them when they are used, and disposing of them properly when recycling is not possible?

> For example, is used motor oil being effectively collected from home mechanics as well as commercial service stations?

> Are CFCs from refrigerators and air conditioners (car as well as building) being recycled?

Water

Water Use. How much water does your overall community use? What is your community's per person water use? How does that compare with the Earth Day goal for total non-agricultural use of less than 230 gallons per person per day by 2000?

> Total Use _____ ; Per Person Use _____

Water Efficiency Assistance Program.

> Does your community have an adequate program that helps households and business improve their water use efficiency?

Sewage Treatment and Water Pollution Control.

> Does your community have adequate programs for preventing water pollution?

Water System Infrastructure.

> Does everyone in your community have good access to safe drinking water?

> Is the water distribution system properly maintained so that no pollution leaks into it and so that no water is wasted through leaky mains?

Energy

Energy Use. How much energy does your overall community use? What is your community's per person energy use? (Local government and local energy companies probably have this information.) How does that compare with the Earth Day goal of less than 12 tons of CO_2 per person per year by 2000?

> Total Use _____ ; Per Person Use _____

Energy Efficiency Assistance Program.

> Does your community have an adequate program (run by local government, a utility company or by an independent group) that helps households and businesses improve their energy efficiency?

Does your community assist business and individuals in shifting to more telecommuting?

Notes

Renewable Energy Sources.

Is your community making good use of sun, wind, hydropower and other renewable energy sources?

Is anyone in your community actively promoting these energy sources to households, businesses, and institutions?

Is anyone actively encouraging your electric utility to invest in renewable sources?

Local Government Energy Use.

Is your local government doing all it can to use energy efficiently in such areas as street lighting, government buildings and government transport?

Are land-use decisions, zoning and other regulations adequately sensitive to their energy-use implications?

Air

Transportation Air Pollution.

How much of the air pollution in your community comes from cars and other motor vehicles?

Are there adequate programs to reduce this source?

Commercial/Industrial Air Pollution.

How much of the air pollution in your community comes from business and industry?

Are there adequate programs to reduce these sources?

Residential Air Pollution.

How much of the air pollution in your community comes from wood smoke and other residential sources?

Are there adequate programs to reduce these sources?

Imported Air Pollution.

How much of the air pollution in your community comes from outside the community?

Are there adequate programs to reduce these sources?

Transportation

Transportation Energy Use. How much transportation energy does your overall community use? What is your community's per person transportation energy use? How does that compare with the Earth Day goal of less than 225 gallons of fuel per person per year by 2000?

Total Use _____ ; Per Person Use _____

What particular species are endangered in your region?

Public Transport.

> Does your community have adequate public transport?

> Are future public transport needs and opportunities being planned for?

Biking & Walking Routes.

> Does your community provide safe routes and other support for non-motorized transportation?

Zoning To Reduce Commuting.

> Do zoning and other regulations make it easy for people to live near where they work?

> Is there support for working at home?

> Do zoning and other regulations encourage a "village" type clustering of stores and offices that reduces the need for car travel?

Species and Habitat Preservation

Pesticides and Toxics.

> Does your community adequately regulate the use of toxic chemicals (including agricultural, lawn and garden chemicals) so that they do not harm the complex web of life in and around your community?

> How does that compare with the Earth Day goal of a 75% reduction in pesticide use by 2000?

Parks and Wilderness.

> Does your community have adequate amounts of, and protection for, open space and wildlife habitat?

> How does that compare with the Earth Day goal of a three-fold increase in ecological preserves by 2000?

Guidelines for Empowering Others

It requires skill to empower others to help heal our Earth. As you might imagine it starts by empowering ourselves and putting our own house in order. Once we have done this we have an authenticity to build from. The following ten guidelines will be useful in helping to empower others.

1) Motivate through creativity not through fear

We need to motivate others through appealing to their creativity rather than through appealing to their fear. Using fear to attempt to bring about change perpetuates more fear in the world, which is the cause of many of the world's problems to start with. When we are afraid we contract, separate and close down. We don't reach out and connect with others. This causes polarization and separation. Using fear is a short-term fix – it may serve as an immediate impetus but is not sustainable over time. Creativity is regenerative; fear is degenerative.

People cannot stay around fear for any length of time. It eats away at their energy and ultimately immobilizes the person psychically. All of the studies have told us that people become numb as a result of appeals through fear. We must motivate people through appealing to their creativity.

2) Concentrate on what you want, not what you don't want

We need to create the new, not just negate the old. It is a time of social creativity. Social protest, even if it doesn't use fear as a motivator, is still a limited model. It doesn't present any alternatives and usually just polarizes. It has its role and

More than just objecting to present conditions and behaviors, we need to put something new in their place.

it needs to go further. Getting rid of a social pathology is just a first step. More than just objecting, we need to put something new in its place. We need to not just reform we need to transform. Otherwise the basic beliefs that caused the social pathology will replicate themselves again.

John Platt in his book *Steps to Man* says: "The main purpose of an enlightened minority is not fighting the majority but showing them how." We need to develop vehicles that elicit social creativity. It is a time for the social entrepreneur to create social innovation, new and imaginative solutions to social problems or unmet social needs. We need to appeal to people's social creativity, inventiveness and ingenuity not their fear, guilt or anger.

It's harder work to motivate by creativity and transform a system or belief. It demands that we have a vision of what we want instead of just a vision of what we don't want. A simple example that illustrates this strategy is a grass-roots organization, CANT – Citizens Against Nuclear Trash. As CANT, the group was unsuccessful in motivating people in Maine; after a name change to Clean Maine, the group became successful.

3) Elicit a vision and provide skills for how to manifest it

People, organizations and communities are more easily motivated to change something if they see they can get what they want by doing it. They are motivated to change something ineffective as a result of a personal desire for something positive that is attractive to them. Help them develop a clear vision of what they'd like to see occur in their life, organization

We're all in this together. We've created this global situation together. We're going to need to change it together.

or community. Then provide them with tools and skills that allow them to manifest that vision. This workbook is an example of a tool for manifesting a vision.

4) Build on what's working

Look for innovation and why it worked. Extract the principles and replicate them. Use role models to empower others to act and draw forth their own social creativity. Make sure information is given so others not only are inspired but are offered "how to" advice they can replicate. These local solutions often become the first step to global solutions.

5) Create desired new behaviors within a part of the community and allow osmosis to take place

This is a slight variation on the previous strategy. Create the new behavior desired in a part of the community. The Household EcoTeam Program is an example. As some members of a community begin adopting environmentally responsible behaviors they model within the community that which ultimately needs to be transferred to the whole community. As success occurs the rest of the community becomes receptive. There is trust because it is happening right within the community. This same strategy works well with a large organization.

The choice of the group to initiate the new behaviors is very important. Work with those who are open to experimentation and can tolerate uncertainty.

6) Create a common ground for agreement

This is a strategy to bring people together of different points of view without polarization. Look for cooperation and common ground and beyond the limitations of "us vs. them." We're all in this together. We've created this planet together. We're going to need to change it together. An example of this is the initiative, In Search of Common Ground, which brings together for example, hawks and doves; Jews and Arabs; pro-life and pro-choice people to search for common ground. As a result they improve their ability to create a dialogue and new avenues for communication open up.

7) To understand the planetary change process link it to the personal

These are some ways to make the social and planetary transformation process accessible to the average person.

–Person ill to planet ill: Person in critical care with his or her vital signs weak to the planet in critical care with its vital signs weak.

–Personal empowerment to planetary empowerment: Take responsibility to create my life as I want it, to take responsibility to create my community or planet as I want it.

–A whole person to a whole planet: To be healthy, we have to be working on body, mind, emotions and spirit. For our planet to be healthy, we have to be working not just on western problems or local problems, but the problems of the whole planet – developed and developing world.

–Personal understanding to cross-cultural understanding: As we get to know another person, we break down that which separates us and appreciate the differences. This same process takes place as we reach out to understand another culture.

Make sure information is given so others not only are inspired but are offered "how to" advice they can replicate.

For people to engage in action over the long-run requires the action be self actualizing.

Since healing
our Earth will
require many
people work-
ing together,
the ability to
bring diverse
groups and
viewpoints
into a common
effort is
essential.

8) Sustainable action for individual needs to further their growth

A sustainable planet comes from sustainable commitment among the people of the planet. For people to engage in action over the long-run requires the action be self actualizing. It has to further them in their own growth, or when time constraints occur, action will get dropped. Help people discover the unique reasons why they are engaging in the action. Reinforce these reasons on a regular basis.

9) Design holistic support systems

Once the transformation process is initiated, people need support to sustain the new behavior and actions. Support systems need to be created around whatever change is initiated. If these are not put into place, commitment will waver. The support system needs to be both outwardly and inwardly relevant. That is, address the content of the changes taking place as well as the individual feelings and struggles the individual is experiencing.

10) Develop synergy

Since healing our Earth will require many people working together, the ability to bring diverse groups and viewpoints into a common effort is essential. Because of competition over financial resources, membership and public visibility among social change groups, this rarely occurs. As a result the overall objectives suffer. Find ways to create situations where all the players win. We must develop a working knowledge of win/win/win agreements – you, me, and the Earth. This is the art of developing strategic alliances.

Note – For practical support in the process of empowering others and in developing the new leadership skills needed for the long-term healing of our Earth, you are invited to participate in GAP's leadership training program. It was specially designed to assist those of us who want to create positive change and transformation in a balanced way. A full description is listed on page 142 in the section of the EcoTeam Workbook entitled "Our Big Picture."

> "Man must cease attributing his problems to his environment, and learn again to exercise his will – his personal responsibility."
> – Albert Schweitzer

Notes for the Coach

Before the monthly meeting

1) Read over this chapter carefully.

2) Prepare for the monthly meeting. Read over the section on "Facilitating an EcoTeam Meeting" on page 8 for general guidelines and suggestions.

3) Make a blank copy of the "Coach's Report" from *each* previous month so that you can use these to record your team's completed carry-over actions.

In the monthly meeting

1) Open the meeting in a way that provides insight into this month's theme.

2) Check-in on experiences and results from the previous month.

3) Gather all the "before" and "after" results for the "Coach's End of Program Report" on page 101.

4) Use the copies of the "Coach's Report" from *each* previous month to record any carry-over actions completed by your team mates. Put all results in the "This Month" column and write "EOP" (for End of Program) after your EcoTeam's registration number at the top of the page.

5) Review with the group the "Action Opportunities" and "Guidelines for Empowering Others" in this chapter.

6) Have a discussion of the possible next steps for each member of the Eco-Team. Options might include:

- Forming a Community EcoTeam with several members or all of the Household EcoTeam. If a Community Eco-Team is already in place, your EcoTeam can assist on the overall program or work on a specific environmental issue that needs action.
- Developing Workplace EcoTeams as individual members
- Activating other Household EcoTeams either as individual members, a sub-group or as a whole group
- Joining an existing environmental group in your community that needs help
- Participating in the leadership training offered by GAP
- Choosing some other expression of concern for the Earth not listed
- Staying together as a support group for long-term household environmental change which could also include supporting any of the above actions team members choose to take
- Bringing closure to the EcoTeam.

7) Support each person in making plans for their next step in caring for the Earth and if the EcoTeam is involved, for its next step.

8) Create a celebration in acknowedgement of what has been achieved and to honor completion of this part of the journey.

After the meeting

Send the "Coach's End of Program Report" and a "Coach's Report" from each previous month that has any completed carry-over actions to the GAP Coordination Office.

Thanks for your part in making this program work, and much success in your next steps!

Our Big Picture

In this section:

About the Global Action Plan
For The Earth

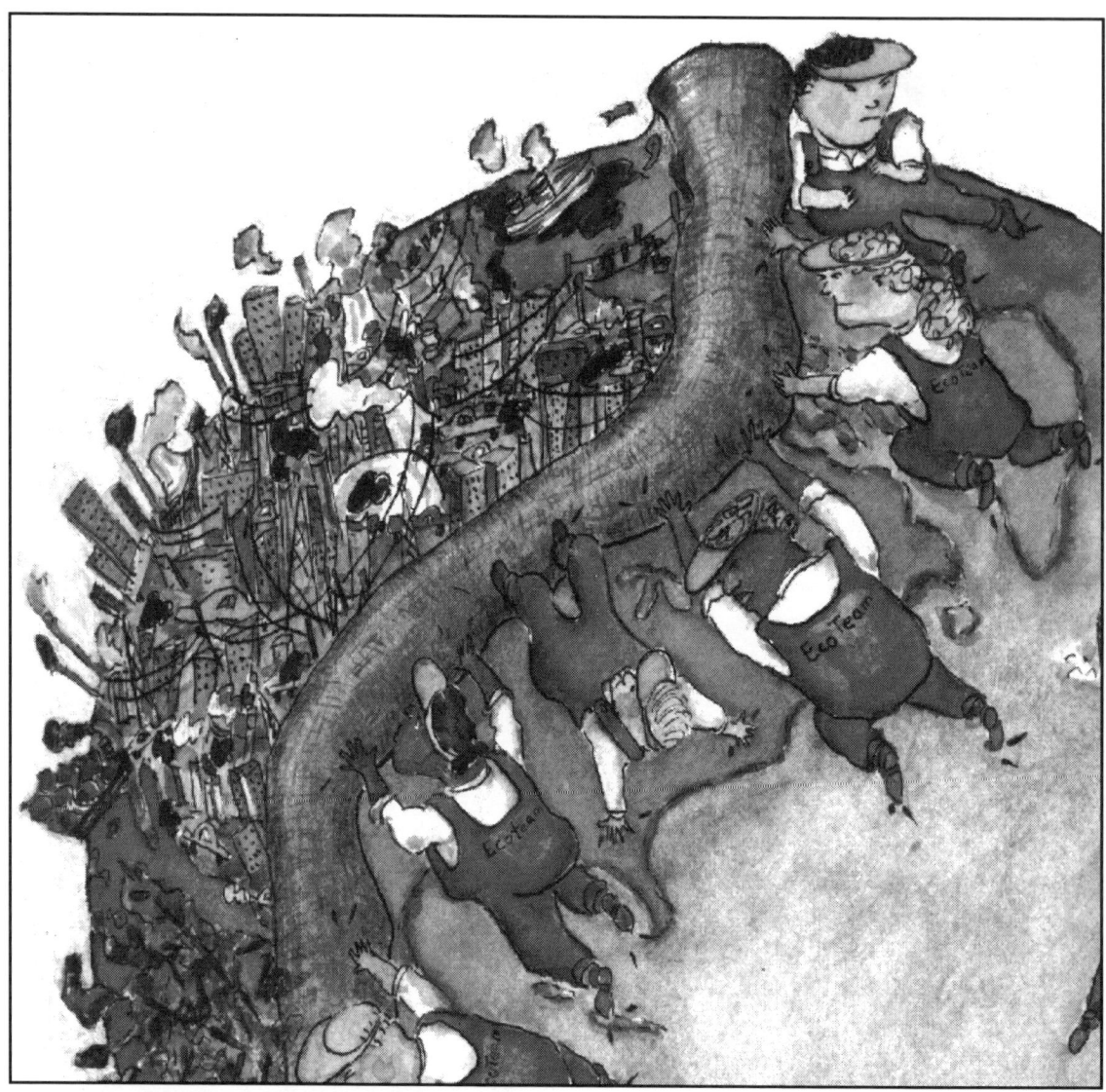

GAP Philosophy

The environmental crisis facing our planet has become an accepted reality worldwide. Our Earth's life support system is unravelling and within the next decade major irreversible damage will occur unless we do something about it. Gerald Barney, author of the *Global 2000 Report* states: "For the first time in history life support systems are being destroyed by human activities threatening the integrity of the whole planet." And Lester Brown in Worldwatch Institute's *State of the World Report* tells us: "We don't have generations, we only have years in which to attempt to turn things around." How do we mobilize ourselves to respond to this extraordinary challenge we are facing?

We need to begin by understanding what in fact is the real environmental problem. It is not primarily pollution, climate change, overpopulation, Third World debt, massive spending on armaments to the detriment of the environment or even greed or selfishness. *It is the belief on a collective level that we can't do anything*

To be motivated to act we must challenge and change the beliefs that disempower us.

about these problems. This belief is encountered all over the world – in the ordinary citizen, grass-roots environmental leader, politician, and business executive alike. It is deeply held in the collective global psyche. Until this belief is changed all our efforts to tackle the specific content problems will be severely hampered.

This belief breaks down into two mutually reinforcing sub-beliefs that disempower the individual, the systems of which they are a part, and consequently the planet at large. The two beliefs are:

- ◆ I don't know how to be effective in changing things
- ◆ The problems are so large that what I do won't make a difference.

As our beliefs determine our actions, to be motivated to act we must challenge and change the beliefs that disempower us. Until these disabling beliefs are transformed, we, the people of our planet, will remain immobilized.

It's important to realize that while pointing out a disabling belief is an important first step this does not by itself transform it. *To transform a belief requires that a person envision the new condition desired and believe it is possible to create it.* In other words as individuals we need a vision of where we are going and we need to believe it is possible to get there before we will be motivated to change our present situation. As soon as we believe our vision can be accomplished we begin to feel hopeful. And to act, we must have hope that our action can bear fruit. This same reasoning applies on a planetary level as well. To be motivated to change our present situation, we need a collective vision around which all members of the human family can align and a rough map for how to achieve it.

The brilliant evolutionary thinker

Teilhard de Chardin many years ago spoke of a moment that would come in which we would have the impetus for a collective vision. He said: "Without any doubt people today suffer and vegetate in isolation; they need a superior impulse to intervene and force them to pass beyond the level at which they are immobilized, leading them to discover their profound affinities. The sense of Earth is the irresistible pressure which will come at the right moment to unite them in a common passion."

This time has come! People are awakened – and the collective vision is saving our Earth from environmental destruction! We have been alerted by scientists from all over the world that we have approximately ten years to restore the health of our planet or much of the deterioration will be irreversible. And people everywhere are responding and looking for a way to act. We have for the first time in our evolution as a human species an issue capable of galvanizing the collective will into a planet-wide concerted action. The environmental crisis has helped us recognize we share a fragile life support system and that the only way we are going to save it and consequently ourselves is by *acting together* to change the way we do things.

Obstacles to Action

Translating the collective vision of saving our Earth into an effective plan of action is the next hurdle we must overcome. In the past many of us have attempted to avoid personal responsibility for action. We have done this through denying there is a problem and looking outside ourselves for the answer. Three of the most widely held beliefs are:

We expect that the planet will just take care of itself without direct intervention. We human beings have created the environmental crisis, it is we who must remedy

> We have been alerted by scientists from all over the world that we have approximately ten years to restore the health of our planet or much of the deterioration will be irreversible.

the situation we've created. Many people have come to understand that an individual who is in a state of disease must take responsibility to change the unhealthy behavior that has led to the disease in order to restore health. If we want to restore our Earth to a healthy state, we need to apply this same lesson. We each need to take responsibility to change our collective unhealthy behaviors that are causing the state of disease.

We expect nation states will "fix it." National leaders are besieged by their various constituencies to solve local and national problems. This leaves them very little time or inclination to focus on the health of the planet as a whole. The responsibility to fill the global leadership vacuum that exists lies with the people of the planet. "When the people lead the leaders will follow." It's up to individuals around the world to develop environmental programs to heal our Earth. Once our programs are demonstrating success we can then as constituents of our various countries motivate our national governments to support these plans with legislation.

We expect the United Nations will "fix it." The United Nations is doing an admirable job framing the global environmental agenda and creating forums for governmental dialogue. Since the UN is a body of nation states, it is influenced by the various political agendas of the different countries. As a result, they have political constraints that limit both their freedom and ability to act with the decisiveness necessary for the environmental crisis we face. What we should expect from the United Nations is that it will act as a planetary information system to provide us with high quality information so we can design educated strategies and plans of action. And, that it supports the initiatives that come from the grass-roots organizations.

> The responsibility to fill the global leadership vacuum that exists lies with the people of the planet.

Mobilizing for Action

Given the impending environmental crisis we face, there are no satisfactory alternatives to not acting. Yet this challenge seems overwhelming. Time magazine in its "Planet of the Year" issue states it most succinctly: "Taking effective action to halt the massive injury being done to the Earth's environment will require a mobilization of political will, international cooperation and sacrifice unknown except in wartime." Since the recourse to avoiding responsibility is unacceptable, we must rise to the occasion.

So how do we mobilize ourselves to act? The clear lessons from decades of experience working on empowerment issues and mobilizing grass-roots activism at a global level are that to be willing to act we need:

- the facts about what is happening to the environment
- the skills and support to be effective
- the knowledge of how our action is making a difference. ·

To accomplish this, a coherent and decentralized global action needs to be created that shows how each action we take, rather than being just a drop in the bucket, is actually filling it up. The Global Action Plan for the Earth (GAP) has been carefully designed to accomplish this objective.

GAP, a non-profit organization formed

GAP is designed to motivate people to act upon their new knowledge.

by a team of experienced international activists, worked with the organizers of Earth Day 1990 to formulate the "Agenda for the Green Decade" – a set of global environmental goals that must be achieved for the Earth to be on a sustainable path. GAP's next step has been to facilitate the achievement of the goals by:

- translating the goals into measurable household, workplace and community actions keyed to the global goals
- providing skills and support systems for achieving these local actions
- collecting the results of these actions and feeding them back to those involved in the program and to the media.

GAP is designed to empower all of us by showing how our individual and local actions are having a global impact, and how it is *precisely* through local action taking place all over the world that we can achieve the global environmental goals necessary to sustain the quality of life on our planet.

The Household EcoTeam Program is the foundation of the Global Action Plan for the Earth. As we learn how to put our individual houses in order, we can, as a next step, apply this knowledge in our workplaces, and then in our communities, until we put our larger home in order.

GAP Strategy

The respected Dutch environmentalist Theo Potma has written that there are five switch-points we must pass through to restore the environment.

I. Consensus on the global environmental threat.

II. Consensus on the solutions needed to respond effectively to the threat.

III. Mobilization to implement the solutions.

IV. Economic accounting that factors in the environmental cost of doing business.

V. Majority of households in environmental balance worldwide.

The industrialized countries are now moving between switch-points two and three:

I	**II GAP III**		**IV**	**V**
Threat	Solutions	Mobilization	Economic	Worldwide

We have reasonable consensus that there is an environmental threat and on what solutions we must implement. The worldwide impact of Earth Day aided in consolidating these first two switch-points. We are now moving into switch-point three – attempting to mobilize ourselves as individuals, communities and businesses to implement the needed solutions. The purpose of the Global Action Plan is to assist in filling the gap between knowing what we need to do and actually getting ourselves to do it. It's designed to motivate people to act upon their new knowledge.

GAP's program starts with the household. At the end of six months the individual household has done those things needed to be in environmental balance and has begun implementing the necessary long term lifestyle changes.

It is precisely through local action taking place all over the world that we can achieve the global environmental goals

One of these new lifestyle patterns is discrimination as to which products and services are environmentally friendly. As household by household starts discriminating about what it buys, in due course what gets manufactured will start to respond to these new purchasing patterns. As the collective impact of these economic votes starts to become substantial, we will move into switch-point four. At this point consumers' environmental consciousness will influence what gets produced and producers will advertise the "green" virtues of their product, which will further raise the environmental consciousness of the consumer. This process is beginning in the United States as evidenced by several recent polls.

Advertising Age magazine reported that 75% of those polled said environmental factors were a criterion for buying a product. A recent *New York Times/CBS News* survey reported in *Fortune* magazine stated that 79% of those polled felt "protecting the environment is so important that requirements and standards could not be set too high and continuing environmental improvements must be made regardless of cost." In that same poll 71% said they were willing to pay higher taxes to clean up the environment.

To further enhance this shift the GAP *Household EcoTeam Workbook* provides specific guidance for those Household Eco-Teams inspired to catalyze changes directly in their workplace and community. As Household EcoTeams educate and empower themselves by putting their own houses in order, many will want to take this to the next level, putting their larger environment – their workplace and community – in order.

Through feedback people begin to see how each action they take, be it at the household, workplace or community level, rather then being "a drop in the bucket," is actually filling it up!

Translating Action into Effective Change

Once people start to do things, they need to know their action is making a difference if they are to continue acting. A *New York Times* article that came out after Earth Day 1990, entitled "People Are Willing to Save the Planet. But How?," says, "now that people are actually taking steps to do their part, they want to be assured that their efforts have an impact... as confusion mounts about just how effective these efforts are the public may become apathetic, disillusioned and turn away."

The first part of the GAP strategy is to assist individuals in translating their awareness into action. The second part is to help the individual sustain a willingness to take action by showing the results of acting. GAP shows the cumulative impact of individual actions through measuring them in relationship to Earth Day's "Agenda for the Green Decade." GAP provides regular feedback on progress being made toward achieving the goals.

Through this feedback people begin to see how each action they take, be it at the household, workplace or community level, rather then being "a drop in the bucket," is actually filling it up! The GAP EcoTeam programs and the numerous actions of the many environmental groups are the drops being measured and the global bucket is Earth Day's "Agenda for the Green Decade."

Timeframe of Action

GAP's timeframe is keyed to the year 2000 – the date "Agenda for the Green Decade" focuses on for achievement of the key global goals. As the last decade of the millennium, the 1990s have taken on a mythic quality. Add to this the predictions of the world's scientists that we need to

As progress is achieved over the decade, more ambitious goals will become possible.

turn things around in this decade or the Earth will go over critical environmental thresholds that are irreversible. GAP will utilize this special timeframe by providing regular reports each Earth Day of progress being made on the global goals and state of mobilization.

The kind of change needed takes time to be instituted. A ten year timeframe for achieving global goals balances flexibility with tension. It provides enough time for our lifestyles and economic system to adapt. As progress is achieved over the decade, more ambitious goals will become possible. It is hoped that GAP's program will help build momentum over time.

Relationship to the Environmental Community

Our primary interface will be with those groups who are involved with direct grass-roots environmental action. GAP will support their initiatives in two ways: By encouraging people who have gone through the Household EcoTeam program to join their efforts, and by inviting these groups to tell us the quantifiable progress they have made toward achieving the global goals so we can feed it back to others to further build momentum. It is our hope that through communicating the results being achieved by these groups in relationship to the global goals, the overall impact of their effort will be more fully valued.

Relationship to the Political Change Process

GAP is based on the premise that when the people lead the leaders will follow. We are focused therefore on those people who are ready to take direct environmental action, which, given the polls, are numerous. As these early innovators demonstrate progress it will ripple out until our political leadership recognizes it is time to act. Legislation at this point will bring along the rest of the members of society who need prodding in order to change. We are also aware that many environmental groups focus on legislation as their change strategy, so in the ecology of action all the pieces will reinforce each other.

Participation in GAP

The following are ways interested individuals can participate in GAP in addition to being part of an EcoTeam:

1) Encourage organizations to which you belong to participate in our organization partnership program. They offer the workbook to their members to help empower them and as a fundraiser for the organization.

2) Encourage your workplace to come into environmental balance by participating in GAP's Corporate Environmental Leadership Program.

3) Use your networks to encourage others to form EcoTeams.

4) Help build the program financially.

For more information on any of the GAP programs, contact: Global Action Plan for the Earth, 84 Yerry Hill Road, Woodstock, NY, 12498, USA; Phone: 914/679-4830, FAX: 914/679-4834.

GAP is inviting grass-roots environmental groups to tell us the quantifiable progress they have made toward achieving the global goals so we can feed it back to others to further build momentum.

Agenda for the Green Decade: Global Environmental Action Goals

At the heart of the Global Action Plan is a set of environmental action goals for the 1990s. The actions you take as part of an EcoTeam enable you to do your part toward the achievement of these goals.

The GAP team worked with the organizers of Earth Day 1990 to formulate a set of global goals that need to be achieved in the next decade in order for the world to enter onto a path of environmental sustainability. What was created and launched by the organizers of Earth Day 1990 was the "Agenda for the Green Decade." The purpose of these global action goals is three-fold:

1) To enable us to know in quantifiable terms what we have to achieve over the next decade to protect the health of our environment. As the old Chinese proverb goes: "If you don't know where you're going there's a good chance you won't get there."

2) To enable us to have reference points for developing and then measuring the progress of our actions. This is the key to building momentum for environmental action in our decade-long campaign to heal the Earth. (As mentioned earlier, GAP's program is built around quantifying the results of actions taken in relationship to these global goals by EcoTeams and environmental groups working on specific issues; then collecting the results and feeding this information back to the Eco-Teams, environmental groups and media.)

3) To serve as a vehicle for alignment among the environmental groups working on the same issue. It is our hope that these groups will use the global goals as a common reference point for discussion, dialogue and cooperation in their areas of mutual interest. Further, it is our hope that they will refine the goals to be most relevant to them.

Since the leverage point for sustainable environmental change is individual lifestyle change, this is where action must begin.

The guidelines used in assembling these goals were that they should:

- address the major environmental issues necessary to restore the health of our environment
- be expressed in quantifiable terms so the results of actions taken can be measured
- be based on the recommendations of the major international commissions and well-recognized institutes
- be keyed to the year 2000, to provide a realistic time frame for mobilizing action and measuring progress.

Several of the items listed in the "Agenda for the Green Decade" focus on political strategies to support the quantifiable environmental objectives. These political goals are not listed here because the purpose of the EcoTeam is direct environmental action. Lobbying is indirect action to get legislation passed to get us to then do something. Direct action means doing it ourselves. Since the leverage point for sustainable environmental change is individual lifestyle change, this is where action must begin. This provides the foundation for influencing legislative change when it's needed.

The goals below are a condensation of the "Agenda for the Green Decade" in a format that is concise and translatable to household, workplace and community actions. The background section provides information on how each goal was derived. The matrices that follow provide the relationship between the local actions and the global goals. The parts of the "Agenda" which are strategy oriented have been integrated directly into the EcoTeam Program.

These goals need to be achieved in the next decade for the world to become environmentally sustainable.

Global Environmental Action Goals To be Achieved by the Year 2000

Preserve the Climate and Atmosphere

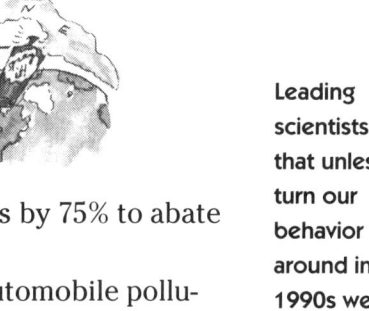

- Decrease carbon dioxide emissions by 20% through increased energy efficiency and increased use of renewable energy sources to slow global warming
- Eliminate emissions of and production of CFCs and other ozone depleting chemicals
- Decrease emissions of sulfur dioxide by 90% and nitrogen oxides by 75% to abate acid rain
- Improve urban air quality in the world's cities by reducing all automobile pollutants at least 50%.

Leading scientists say that unless we turn our behavior around in the 1990s we may well push the environment beyond the point where reversal is possible.

Preserve Biological Diversity

- Triple the area of protected ecological preserves for species preservation
- Reduce deforestation by 50%
- Increase reforestation enough to offset deforestation by planting 100 billion trees
- Shift 50% of agricultural production to low-input sustainable agriculture. Reduce global pesticide use by 75%.

Reduce Waste

- Reduce solid waste by 75% through recycling, source reduction and composting
- Cut the production of hazardous waste by 80%
- Clean up all existing toxic, hazardous and nuclear waste sites to acceptable levels of safety.

Use Water Wisely

- Reduce water use by a third or more through more efficient use in agriculture, industry, and households
- Provide safe drinking water for all.

Stabilize Humanity

- Reduce the rate of world population growth by 50%
- Eliminate hunger.

The Background for the Goals

This section describes each of the goals in more detail and provides background information as well as references for their sources.

Preserve the Climate and Atmosphere

Humankind is fouling the atmosphere at an alarming rate. Smog and acid rain have already damaged regional areas all around the world. The prospects of global warming (leading to major climate change and rising sea levels) and ozone depletion (leading at least to higher skin cancer rates and possibly to the destruction of major biological food chains) gets closer every day. That's the bad news. The good news is that since these are all caused by human actions they can all be turned around by human action. But we don't have much time. Leading scientists say that unless we turn our behavior around in the 1990s we may well push the environment beyond the point where reversal is still possible.

Goal 1: Decrease carbon dioxide emissions by 20% through increased energy efficiency and increased use of renewable energy sources to slow global warming. Many gases contribute to global warming, but the most important is carbon dioxide (CO_2). About 3/4 of the excess CO_2 now building up in the atmosphere comes from the burning of oil, coal and natural gas (fossil fuels) while the rest comes from the removal of trees that normally absorb CO_2 (deforestation).[1] In this goal we address the need to turn the current 3% per year growth in CO_2 emission into a 3% per year decline.

Why 20%? Scientists from the the US Environmental Protection Agency estimate that stabilizing CO_2 at current levels would require a 50-80% reduction in emissions, but it is unlikely that such a major reduction could be achieved by 2000. Most analysts see the 50 to 80% target as a goal for 2030 or later. The 20% figure for 2000 is a recommendation from the Worldwatch Institute,[2] based on the results from the June 1988 meeting of scientists and environmental policy makers in Toronto. It is clearly a minimum target that will need to be surpassed in the coming decades.

To achieve the 20% goal and further reductions, the wealthy quarter of the world's population – that currently accounts for 70% of the CO_2 emissions from fossil fuels – has a clear responsibility to make a proportionally larger reduction. Thus the Green Agenda, in agreement with Worldwatch, recommends the following in the US by the year 2000: per capita home energy use be reduced by 30%, industrial and commercial energy use by 35% and transportation energy use by 40%.

Goal 2: Eliminate emissions of and production of CFCs and other ozone depleting chemicals. Chlorofluorocarbons, better known as CFCs, are a group of industrial chemicals that are used in refrigerators and air conditioners, in the manufacture of various plastic foams, and as solvents in the electronics industry. Until recently they were thought to be totally harmless, but in the past few years it has become clear that they are 1) a major cause of the loss of high-altitude ozone (that shields us from cancer-causing ultraviolet) and 2) a major greenhouse gas (responsible for about 25% of the total global warming now, and with a use rate growing much faster than CO_2).

Alternative chemicals exist for all the uses that CFCs currently serve and there is now wide international consensus that

> To achieve the 20% goal and further reductions, the wealthy quarter of the world's population – that currently accounts for 70% of the CO2 emissions from fossil fuels – has a clear responsibility to take the lead.

Preventing the leakage of CFCs from refrigerators depends on broad grass-roots awareness and action.

CFC production should be eliminated. In the 1987 Montreal Protocol, the major CFC producing nations agreed to cut production in half by 2000, but this is now seen as inadequate. The Green Agenda goal of the complete elimination of CFC production by 2000 reflects current international environmental opinion.[3]

Production is only half the battle. Even if production stopped today there is still a huge quantity of CFCs in refrigerators and other products that needs to be prevented from leaking into the atmosphere. This prevention depends on broad grass-roots awareness and action.

Goal 3: Decrease emissions of sulfur dioxide by 90% and nitrogen oxides by 75% to abate acid rain. Human produced sulfur dioxide (SO_2) and nitrogen oxides (NO_x) are the sources of acid rain, a form of pollution that is destroying lakes and forests, decreasing the productivity of agricultural land, eroding historic buildings all over the world, and attacking human health.

Sulfur dioxide is primarily a product of burning coal. Current "scrubber" technologies can remove up to 95% of SO_2 from the smokestacks of power plants and factories, the prime sources of SO_2. Nitrogen oxides are produced in the burning of all fossil fuels. About half of the current emissions come from motor vehicles, a third comes from power plants, and the rest from industry. Nitrogen oxides also contribute to global warming (currently 6% of the total effect) and to the destruction of the ozone layer. NO_x emissions can be reduced by a variety of technologies, and both SO_2 and NO_x can be reduced by improving energy efficiency.

The Green Agenda goals of a 90% reduction for SO_2 and 75% for NO_x are based on estimates of the reduction in acid rain required to save forest and lake ecosystems[4] and what is currently technologically feasible.

Goal 4: Improve urban air quality in the world's major cities by reducing all automobile pollutants at least 50%. The damage done to human health and the environment by motor vehicle air pollution is enormous, not only in the industrialized countries, but increasingly in developing countries as well. The level of this pollution could be significantly reduced by a combination of better transportation alternatives (from public transport to bicycles), higher efficiency vehicles, and tighter emission controls.

Preserve Biological Diversity

It has taken the Earth 4.5 billion years to produce today's intricate web of life with its millions of species – a truly priceless heritage. Yet unless we change direction current estimates are that human activities will be responsible for the extinction of 10% of all these species by 2000 and 25% of all of them by 2020. What took millions and billions of years to produce will be wiped out by our carelessness in only a few decades. Much of this loss is taking place in the tropics where species diversity is the greatest and where human population and environmental destruction are expanding at the most rapid rate.

What do we lose when a species becomes extinct? We may never know the whole story, but we do know that our agriculture, our medicine and our industry all depend in critical ways on species from all over the world, and we will continue to depend on them into the foreseeable future. For example, over 40% of the prescription drugs sold in the US are derived from wild species.[4] How many new cures and new foods will we lose during the extinction of the next few decades?

It has taken the Earth 4.5 billion years to produce today's intricate web of life with its millions of species – a truly priceless heritage.

Our agriculture, our medicine and our industry all depend in critical ways on species from all over the world

In addition, the web of life is intricately interdependent. The loss of critical groups of organisms within a food chain can cause a whole ecosystem to collapse, or a previously controlled species to become a highly destructive, ravaging pest. In the past the natural pace of extinction was generally so slow that ecosystems could make evolutionary adjustments. In the few cases where change was rapid, as in the extinction of the dinosaurs 65 million years ago, mass extinction and ecosystem collapse was a major feature. Today's pace is so rapid that biological adjustment is impossible and unpredictable collapse all too probable.

And finally, who are we to perpetrate this genocide against millions of our fellow species?

Today's major sources of species extinction are:[6]

♦ loss of wild habitat, especially in the tropics and in wetlands like swamps and estuaries

♦ competition with non-native species imported by human activities

♦ excessive harvesting, especially of large animals like elephants and whales.

Goal 5: Triple the area of protected ecological preserves for species preservation.[7] The only fundamental way to preserve life's biological diversity is to make sure all species have a place to live. For many species that means true wilderness.

Goals 6 and 7: Reduce deforestation by 50%.[8] *Increase reforestation enough to offset deforestation by planting 100 billion trees.*[9] Deforestation is probably the number one cause of species extinction through habitat loss. The only way to turn this around is to at least slow the rate of cutting in current forests and at least stabilize overall forest area through tree planting.

Goal 8: Shift 50% of agricultural production to low-input sustainable agriculture. Reduce global pesticide use by 75%. Agricultural land used to provide a habitat for vast numbers of species, from birds and small mammals to the microbes in the soil. Today, chemical farming has turned agricultural land into sterile deserts supporting only a few crop species. Low-chemical-input sustainable agriculture is producing high farm yields at reduced costs by working with natural ecosystems instead of against them. In the process, this approach also greatly reduces the energy use and the pollution impact of farming. The 50% shift reflects the Green Agenda's estimate of an achievable goal, given the current rapid increase in interest in low-input sustainable agriculture as farmers all around the world confront the rising costs and ecological consequences of chemical farming.

Reduce Waste

Our industrial society thinks in one-way terms, but nature works in cycles. We dig up minerals that have been concentrated into usable ore through millions of years of geological processes, use them for a few minutes or a few years, then mix them into a toxic stew called "garbage" and bury them in a landfill where they will remain useless (or worse) into the indefinite future. In nature, on the other hand, the waste from one process or species is usually the food or raw material for another. The form keeps changing but the underlying material is reused again and again.

Our failure to follow the principles of nature is costing us dearly and will bankrupt us before long. Not only are we using

up precious materials at an alarming rate, but we are also running out of places to put our garbage. In the 10 years from 1978 to 1988 the number of landfills in the US dropped from 20,000 to 6,000.[10] The only sustainable solution to our dilemma is to follow nature's lead by reorienting our economy to extensive reuse and recycling.

Goal 9: Reduce solid waste by 75% through source reduction, recycling, and composting.[11] Reuse and recycling not only save landfill space, they save energy and thus reduce air pollution, and they reduce the disruption of natural habitats and pollution caused by mining, logging and primary manufacturing. Can we achieve the 75% goal by 2000? Even in the mid-1980s, Japan was sending only 27% of its solid waste to landfills.[12]

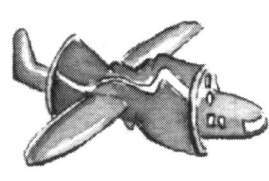

Goal 10: Cut the production of hazardous waste by 80%.[13] Much of our waste is more than just a squandering of resources, energy and land. It is actually dangerous and capable of poisoning water, soil and air. The quantity of hazardous material that needs to be disposed of as waste (about 1 ton per person per year in the US[14]) can be greatly reduced by substituting less toxic alternatives, by recycling toxic industrial chemicals, and by treating wastes before disposal to make them less toxic. There are a wide and growing range of technologies for this; there are even special strains of bacteria that can break down various toxic chemicals.

Goal 11: Clean up all existing toxic, hazardous and nuclear waste sites to acceptable levels of safety. Unsafe hazardous waste sites threaten air, soils and water. Especially worrisome is the poisoning of groundwater supplies which, once done,

is not repairable. We must avert this catastrophe.

Use Water Wisely

Clean water is essential to life. Unfortunately, all over the world supplies of fresh water are being squeezed between growing demand from agriculture, industry and households and growing pollution that makes existing supplies less and less usable. Many parts of the world have run out of new sources to tap. The only real solution is to use water more efficiently and keep it clean so that it can be used and reused.

In addition, the human use of water resources is intimately connected to many other environmental issues. Dams, river diversions and other large water projects frequently disrupt natural habitats and contribute to species extinction. The pumping, heating, and purifying of water uses large amounts of energy, thereby contributing to global air pollution. In many parts of the world, poorly managed irrigation projects have built up so much salt in the soil that the land has become useless. Again, the only real way to avoid aggravating these other environmental problems is to use water more efficiently and keep it clean so that it can be used and reused.

Goal 12: Reduce water use by a third or more through more efficient use in agriculture, industry, and households.[15] More so than with the other goals on this list, the 1/3 reduction should be seen as an average figure that needs to be adjusted to local conditions. Different regions of the world vary considerably in their need for better water conservation, although even water-rich regions can benefit from the energy and habitat savings that come with less water use.

Low-chemical-input sustainable agriculture is producing high farm yields at reduced costs by working with natural ecosystems instead of against them.

Goal 13: Provide safe drinking water for all.[16] About a quarter of the world's population lacks access to safe drinking water, and even in industrialized countries supposedly safe water contains an increasing variety of chemical pollutants whose effect on human health is poorly understood. In less developed countries polluted water is a major source of infant mortality and debilitating diseases, both of which ironically contribute to rapid population growth and further environmental destruction. In addition to its obvious human benefits, this goal provides a necessary minimum standard for the reduction and elimination of all forms of water pollution.

Stabilize Humanity

Everything that is normally described as an "environmental" problem could be more accurately called an environmental symptom of a human problem. Many of these symptoms can be alleviated by using more efficient and cleaner technologies, but unless we can stop population growth even the best technologies will soon be overwhelmed.

And while most environmental problems are caused by the wealthy quarter of the world's population living in industrialized countries, problems such as tropical deforestation are made worse by the struggle of hundreds of millions of the desperately poor to survive. Likewise, desperate poverty feeds social instability, which fuels arms races, which diverts much needed funds away from improving social conditions, which leads to further poverty along a descending spiral of social and ecological collapse. We have reached the point where we can no longer afford the high environmental cost of poverty.[17]

Goal 14: Reduce the rate of world population growth by 50%.[18] All of the wealthy industrialized countries have population growth rates below 1% per year. All of the poor countries have growth rates over 2%. Can these high rates be cut in half? Japan did just this between 1949 and 1956, laying important groundwork for its later economic success. Two decades later China made a similar cut. With a 50% decline in population growth by the year 2000, and further declines beyond, we have hope of stabilizing the world's population at or below 8 billion some time in the first half of the 21st century. Such a stabilization is absolutely essential for restoring the world's environment to ecological health.

Goal 15: Eliminate hunger.[19] Hunger is perhaps the most meaningful measure of poverty – the kind of poverty that drives both social instability and ecological destruction. We have the technical means to end hunger; what is needed is the social will. The creative energy released by eliminating hunger may turn out to be one of the essential keys to returning our planet to environmental balance.

The Goals and You

Viewed at a global level these goals easily seem overwhelming, well beyond anything you could hope to affect, but this disempowering impression is an illusion. The illusion is fed by two assumptions we often unconsciously carry – that we need to do this task all by ourselves and that we need to do it immediately. In fact, you only need to do your part and you have a decade to accomplish these goals. As this workbook shows, it is surprisingly easy to achieve, and often surpass, these goals in your own life, many of them in less than a year.

> Everything that is normally described as an "environmental" problem could be more accurately called an environmental symptom of a human problem.

We can no longer afford the high environmental cost of poverty.

Endnotes:

1   Christopher Flavin, Slowing Global Warming: A Worldwide Strategy, *Worldwatch Paper 91*, October 1989, p. 13.

2   Lester R. Brown, *et al., State of the World 1990*, (New York: WW Norton & Co., 1990) p. 34.

3   *ibid*, p. 35.

4   *ibid*, p.116.

5   Walter H. Corson (ed), *The Global Ecology Handbook*, (Boston: Beacon Press, 1990) p. 103.

6   *ibid*, p.101.

7   World Commission on Environment and Development (Gro Harlem Brundtland, Chairman), *Our Common Future*, (New York: Oxford University Press, 1987), p.166.

8   Lester R. Brown, *et al., State of the World 1989*, (New York: WW Norton & Co., 1989) p. 182.

9   *ibid*, p. 181.

10 Walter H. Corson, *op. cit.*, p.266.

11 Renew America, State of the States, 1987, p. 17.

12 Walter H. Corson, *op. cit.*, p.270.

13 Lester R. Brown, *et al., State of the World 1988*, (New York: WW Norton & Co., 1988) p. 118.

14 Walter H. Corson, *op. cit.*, p. 246.

15 Lester R. Brown, *et al., State of the World 1985*, (New York: WW Norton & Co., 1985) p. 50-66.

16 United Nations Environment Programme, press release, October 17, 1985. Walter H. Corson, *op. cit.*, p. 163.

17 Lester R. Brown *et al.,* 1990, *op. cit.*, p. 153.

18 Lester R. Brown *et al.,* 1989, *op. cit.*, p. 190.

19 United Nations Environment Programme (UNEP), *Global Perspectives to the Year 2000*, p. 10.

We have the technical means to end hunger; what is needed is the social will.

Interaction Matrix between the Global Goals and the Household/Personal Action Areas

Action Area	Preserve Climate & Atmosphere	Decrease CO_2 emissions	Eliminate CFCs	Decrease SO_2 and NO_x	Decrease urban auto pollution	Preserve Biological Diversity	Triple eco-preserves	Reduce deforestation	Increase reforestation	Shift to sustainable agriculture	Reduce Waste	Reduce solid waste volume	Cut hazardous waste production	Clean up toxic dumps	Use Water Wisely	Reduce water use	Keep water clean	Stabilize Humanity	Reduce population growth	Eliminate hunger
Garbage																				
Reduce your input	X	X					X	X				X	X				X			
Reuse	X	X						X				X	X				X			
Recycle	X	X						X				X	X				X			
Handle toxics with care		X											X				X			
Water																				
Toilet						X										X	X			
Shower	X	X		X												X	X			
Faucets	X	X		X												X	X			
Appliances	X	X		X												X	X			
Yard watering						X										X	X			
Energy																				
Heating & cooling	X	X																		
Hot water	X	X														X				
Appliances	X	X	X																	
Lighting	X	X																		
Transportation																				
Reduce your need	X			X	X							X				X				
Use alternatives	X			X	X							X				X				
More efficient car	X	X		X	X							X				X				
Eco-wise Consumer																				
Bulk, direct & local	X	X	X	X			X	X		X		X	X						X	X
Keep it maintained	X	X	X	X								X	X							
Eat low on the food chain	X	X	X	X			X	X		X		X	X			X	X		X	X
Grow your own food	X	X	X	X			X	X	X	X		X	X						X	X

Interaction Matrix between the Global Goals and the Workplace Action Areas

	Preserve Climate & Atmosphere	Decrease CO_2 emissions	Eliminate CFCs	Decrease SO_2 and NO_x	Decrease urban auto pollution	Preserve Biological Diversity	Triple eco-preserves	Reduce deforestation	Increase reforestation	Shift to sustainable agriculture	Reduce Waste	Reduce solid waste volume	Cut hazardous waste production	Clean up toxic dumps	Use Water Wisely	Reduce water use	Keep water clean	Stabilize Humanity	Reduce population growth	Eliminate hunger
Waste																				
Paper	X	X						X				X	X				X			
Recycling	X	X						X				X	X				X			
Hazardous Materials		X											X				X			
Water																				
For Employees	X	X		X												X	X			
Washing	X	X		X												X	X			
Production	X	X		X												X	X			
Energy																				
Heating & cooling	X	X																		
Hot water	X	X														X				
Equipment	X	X	X																	
Lighting	X	X																		
Transportation																				
Employee commuting	X			X	X							X					X			
Business travel	X			X	X							X					X			
Shipping & receiving	X			X	X							X					X			
Eco-wise Production																				
Lifecycle design	X	X	X					X				X	X			X	X			
Packaging	X	X	X					X				X	X							
Servicing	X	X	X					X				X	X			X	X			
Eco-wise Purchasing																				
Purchasing Awareness	X	X	X				X	X	X	X		X	X			X	X		X	X

Interaction Matrix between the Global Goals and the Community Action Areas

Community Action Areas	Preserve Climate & Atmosphere	Decrease CO_2 emissions	Eliminate CFCs	Decrease SO_2 and NO_x	Decrease urban auto pollution	Preserve Biological Diversity	Triple eco-preserves	Reduce deforestation	Increase reforestation	Shift to sustainable agriculture	Reduce Waste	Reduce solid waste volume	Cut hazardous waste production	Clean up toxic dumps	Use Water Wisely	Reduce water use	Keep water clean	Stabilize Humanity	Reduce population growth	Eliminate hunger
Waste																				
Recycling	X	X				X						X	X			X	X			
Hazardous Materials			X										X	X			X			
Water																				
Water Efficiency Program	X	X				X										X	X			
Water Pollution Control																	X			
Infrastructure	X	X				X										X	X			
Energy																				
Energy Efficiency Program	X	X																		
Renewable Energy Sources	X	X																		
Local Government Use	X	X																		
Air Pollution																				
Transportation		X		X																
Commercial/Industrial		X	X																	
Residential	X	X																		
Imported			X	X																
Transportation																				
Public Transport	X			X	X								X				X			
Biking & Walking	X			X	X								X				X			
Zoning & Land Use	X			X	X								X				X			
Habitat																				
Pesticides & Toxics						X							X				X			
Parks & Wilderness						X	X	X												

Bibliography & Resources

Publications:

Berry, Thomas. *The Dream of the Earth.* San Francisco: Sierra Club Books, 1988.

Brown, Lester R., *et al., State of the World 1990.* New York: Norton, 1990.

Caplan, Ruth. *Our Earth, Ourselves.* New York: Bantam Books, 1990.

Commoner, Barry. *Making Peace with the Planet.* New York: Pantheon, 1990.

Corson, Walter H., ed. *The Global Strategy Handbook.* Boston: Beacon Press, 1990.

EarthWorks Group. *50 Simple Things Kids Can Do To Save The Earth.* Berkeley: Earthworks Press, 1990.

EarthWorks Group. *50 Simple Things You Can Do To Save The Earth.* Berkeley:Earthworks Press, 1989.

Erickson, Brad. *Call to Action: Handbook for Ecology.* San Francisco: Sierra Club Books, 1990.

Gershon, David and Gail Straub. *Empowerment: The Art of Creating Your Life as You Want It.* New York: Dell, 1989.

Gildred, Kathleen. *Personal Action Guide For The Earth,* Santa Monica, CA: The Transmissions Project of the UN Environment Program, 1989.

Hanhart, Jan. *Ecofeedback: Feedback as a tool in restoring environmental and humanitarian equilibrium.* Rosalen, The Netherlands: Publiek Ontwerp BV, 1989.

Hassol, Susan and Beth Richman. *Creating a Healthy World: 101 Practical Tips for Home and Work.* Snowmass, CO: The Windstar Foundation, 1989.

Hollender, Jeffrey. *How to Make the World a Better Place: A Guide to Doing Good.* New York: William Morrow, 1990.

Lamb, Marjorie. *2 Minutes a Day for a Greener Planet.* New York: Harper & Row, 1990.

MacEachern, Diane. *Save Our Planet: 750 Everyday Ways You Can Help Clean Up the Earth.* New York: Dell, 1990.

Moosewood Collective, The. *New Recipes from Moosewood Restaurant.* Berkeley: Ten Speed Press, 1987.

Naar, John. *Design for a Livable Planet.* New York: Harper and Row, 1990.

Rifkin, Jeremy, ed. *The Green Lifestyle Handbook.* New York: Henry Holt & Co., 1989.

Robinson, Laurel, Carol Flinders, and Bronwen Godfrey. *Laurel's Kitchen.* Petaluma, CA: Nilgiri Press, 1976.

Robbins, John. *Diet for a New America.* Walpole, NH: Stillpoint Pub., 1987.

Steger, Will and Jon Bowermaster. *Saving the Earth: A Citizen's Guide to Environmental Action.* New York: Alfred A. Knopf, 1990.

The Energy Saver's Handbook: For Town and City People. Emmaus: Rodale Press, 1982.

Will, Rosalyn, et.al. *Shopping for a Better World: A Quick and Easy Guide to Socially Responsible Supermarket Shopping.* New York: Council on Economic Priorities, 1989.

Mail-Order Sources for water-saving and energy-saving equipment:

Jade Mountain, PO Box 4616, Boulder, CO 80306, 303/449-6601.

Real Goods Trading Company, 966 Mazzoni Street, Ukiah, CA 95482, 1-800-762-7325.

Seventh Generation, Colchester, VT 05446, 1-800-456-1177.

Planetary Solutions, 1332 Pearl Street, Boulder, CO 80302, 303/444-1088.

Leadership Training

This training is for those who recognize something new is needed and are not satisfied to remain passive.

Come ready to stretch your vision of yourself and what's possible for our planet!

GAP is aware that to bring about change in our workplaces and communities requires individuals who are willing to take leadership roles. It is also aware that a new approach to leadership is necessary – one that is about empowerment, transformation and vision. The new approach must balance the inner development of the leader with the outer skills necessary to bring about results. Leadership is not about controlling others but releasing their full potential. Without this new kind of leadership the changes we want to bring about will not be sustainable. To support this process a very special training program was designed and is available to all those who want to develop or refine their abilities within this new leadership paradigm. A description of the training follows.

FIRE IN THE SOUL
The Path of Transformative Leadership

With the rapid acceleration of change and breakdown of our institutions and environment, we are being challenged in the nineties to fundamentally re-envisage how we think and do things. Given the magnitude of incoherence between what is and what is needed, fixing and reforming isn't a satisfactory change strategy. Nothing short of a transformation of our organizations, communities and planet at large into something that doesn't presently exist, something totally new will suffice. To accomplish this a new kind of leadership must be developed – one able to both envision the new and skillful enough to guide others through the transformation that accompanies such dramatic change. In short, a leadership knowledgeable in

Change in our workplaces and communities requires individuals who are willing to take leadership roles.

the methodology and strategies of transformation. This training provides a map, compass and fire for the soul to those venturing in the uncharted territory of transformative change.

Fire in the Soul draws upon David's two decades of transformative leadership experience as organizer of the First Earth Run, the Global Action Plan and leader of personal and organizational empowerment trainings. If you're in management, consulting or social/environmental/cultural change activities this training will provide you with the essential skills necessary to bring about the transformative change you are seeking to initiate. It will help you cultivate the inner strength and clarity to confidently overcome the challenges. And it will ennoble your core impulse as a pathfinder of the new dream.

This training in transformative leadership can best be described as a hero or heroine's journey, not unlike the transformative process one goes through to effect change in the world. The training is divided into four stages that build upon each other.

Gathering Power

You will learn how to shift your gaze from pathology to vision; transform resistances you have to engaging in transformative action; manifest what you want; and accelerate your growth process.

The Vision Quest

You will explore your deeper calling; develop a vision for your transformative work that allows you to self actualize through its implementation; gain insight into three primary drivers of evolution on the planet – environmental concern,

earth-based spirituality and empowerment of the individual; and align your vision with the needs of the planet.

Transformative Leadership Training

Working with the leadership archetypes of the magician healer and spiritual warrior you will learn strategies that accelerate transformative change with individuals, organizations and systems; strategies that elicit cooperation and create synergy; and how to cultivate within you the qualities of the magician healer and spiritual warrior.

Initiation

You will go through a mythic initiation in which you and the community with which you have journeyed apply the transformative leadership skills and knowledge gained through the training.

Come ready for an adventure! Come ready to stretch your vision of yourself and what's possible for our planet! Come ready to engage in the high play of our time – evolving our world!

Note

This training was created and is led by David Gershon. The hours are Thursday evening 7:00-10:30 pm, Friday and Saturday 9:00 am-10:30 pm, and Sunday 9:00 am-8:00 pm.

For information about dates, tuition and locations contact: Global Action Plan for the Earth, 84 Yerry Hill Road, Woodstock, New York 12498, USA; Phone: (914) 679-4830; Fax: (914) 679-4834.

This training will provide a vehicle for participants to cross-pollinate ideas and strategies; refine skills and enhance effectiveness; deepen personal growth and create a global context for their action.

About the Authors

David Gershon is founder and President of the Global Action Plan for the Earth. He has developed and led empowerment training programs at the individual, corporate, and community level for two decades. He is author of *Empowerment: The Art of Creating Your Life As You Want It*, published by Dell.

David applied his knowledge of empowerment globally as organizer of First Earth Run – the world's largest mass participation peace event. The First Earth Run took place in 1986 under the banner of the United Nations Year of Peace. A lighted torch was passed through sixty-two countries, encircling the planet with light. Twenty-five million people and forty-five heads-of-state participated in this celebration of our possibility to live in harmony with each other and the Earth. The torch also shed light on what was working in the world – hundreds of community self-help initiatives making a difference. The First Earth Run raised several million dollars that were distributed through its sponsor, UNICEF, to the neediest children on our planet. ABC television provided weekly coverage of this epic twelve-week, around-the-world journey. Through the global media 500 million people were made aware of the Earth Run.

Robert Gilman is Director and co-founder of the Context Institute. He is an authority on many aspects of creating a sustainable future including low-environmental-impact lifestyles and strategies for cultural change. He is also the founding editor of the internationally acclaimed journal, *IN CONTEXT, A Quarterly of Humane Sustainable Culture*. This journal, now in its eighth year, is available from the Context Institute, PO Box 11470, Bainbridge Island, WA 98110 for $18 per year.

His work with GAP has included development of the global environmental goals on which the "Agenda for the Green Decade" is based, collaboration on the development of the Household EcoTeam Program, and assisting the international development of GAP.

Robert received a B.A. in astronomy from the University of California (Berkeley) and a Ph.D. in astrophysics from Princeton University. He taught at the University of Minnesota and served as a Research Fellow at the Harvard Smithsonian Astrophysical Observatory, as well as a Research Associate at NASA's Institute for Space Studies, before he decided 15 years ago that "the stars could wait but the planet couldn't."

Household EcoTeam Workbook
Order Form

I would like to order _____ Household EcoTeam Workbook(s)
at $14.95 each plus shipping and handling. (Shipping and handling rates:
$2.50 for 1, $4.50 per order for 2 to 5 copies, and $7.50 for 6 to 10.
Contact us for rates on larger orders.)

_____ Workbooks x $14.95 = $_____
shipping and handling = $_____
subtotal = $_____
NY state residents add appropriate county sales tax: $_____
total enclosed: $_____

Please send these Household EcoTeam Workbook(s) to :

Name: _____

Address: _____

_____

Phone: _____

(designate day or evening phone)

_____ *Yes! I am starting an EcoTeam. Please send me the EcoTeam Start-up information I'll need to tap into the feedback system.*

Please make checks payable to:
Global Action Plan
84 Yerry Hill Road, Woodstock, NY 12498
Phone: 914/679-4830; FAX: 914/679-4834

- -

Please send information about the Household EcoTeam Program and
Global Action Plan for the Earth to:

Name: _____

Address: _____

_____

Name: _____

Address: _____